מסורה

ArtScroll Youth Series®

TALES OF

by G. MaTov

translated by
Shaindel Weinbach

illustrated by
Miriam Bardugo

TZADDIKIM

A wonderful collection of stories from our Sages
and the great Torah and Chassidic leaders,
arranged according to the Sidra of the week.

Published by

Mesorah Publications, ltd

in conjunction with

HAMESORAH /
Jerusalem

FIRST EDITION
First Impression . . . October 1988
SECOND EDITION
First Impression . . . January 1999
Second Impression . . . January 2001

Published and Distributed by
MESORAH PUBLICATIONS, Ltd.
4401 Second Avenue
Brooklyn, New York 11232

Distributed in Europe by
LEHMANNS
Unit E, Viking Industrial Park
Rolling Mill Road
Jarrow, Tyne & Wear NE32 3DP
England

Distributed in Australia & Zew Zealand b,
GOLDS WORLD OF JUDAICA
3-13 William Street
Balaclava, Melbourne 3183
Victoria Australia

Distributed in Israel by
SIFRIATI / A. GITLER — BOOKS
6 Hayarkon Street
Bnei Brak 51127

Distributed in South Africa by
KOLLEL BOOKSHOP
Shop 8A Norwood Hypermarket
Norwood 2196, Johannesburg, South Africa

THE ARTSCROLL YOUTH SERIES®
TALES OF TZADDIKIM / VOL. ii — SHEMOS

4401 Second Avenue / Brooklyn, N.Y. 11232 / (718) 921-9000 / www.artscroll.com

ISBN:
0-89906-827-8 (hard cover)

Printed in the United States of America by Noble Book Press Corp.
Bound by Sefercraft Quality Bookbinders, Ltd., Brooklyn, N.Y.

Table of Contents

◆§ Parashas Sh'mos

◆§ Parashas Va'eyra

◆§ Parashas Bo

◆ Parashas Beshalach

◆ Parashas Yisro

◆ Parashas Mishpatim

◆§ Parashas Terumah

◆§ Parashas Tetzaveh

◆§ Parashas Ki Sisa

Tales of Tzaddikim

פָּרָשַׁת שְׁמוֹת

Parashas Sh'mos

Where The Road Begins

וַתֵּלֶד בֵּן וַתֵּרֶא אֹתוֹ כִּי־טוֹב הוּא

And she gave birth to a son and she saw him that he was good (2:2)

When Moshe was born the entire house filled with light.
(Rashi)

The Sefas Emes, as the second Gerrer Rebbe was called, was very young when he became Admor of the Gerrer chasidim. Some were disturbed by his youth. "How can such a young man lead Jews twice and three times his age, men who are noted scholars and famed for their piety?" they wondered.

One of the chasidim answered the question by the use of a parable:

A man who lived at the foot of a high mountain had always desired to climb all the way to the top. One day he decided that the time had come to realize his lifetime dream. He looked up at the cloud-encircled peak and began climbing. He walked with a sure foot, invigorated by the thought that his dream would soon come true.

He walked for one day and then another. He looked back and saw that he had come a long way, yet, when he looked up at the mountain peak, it seemed as distant as ever. But he did not get discouraged. He knew that as long as he kept on walking, he would be nearing his goal. The man walked at a steady pace, day after day. Still, the distance hardly seemed less.

Weeks passed and he was still far from his destination which towered majestically above him. Still, he trudged steadily onwards towards his goal. The weeks turned into months, the months became years; the man pressed on. This was his lifetime dream and he refused to turn back now, after he had come all this way.

Finally, after years of constant, tireless effort, he saw the mountain peak looming up right before his eyes. Soon, soon he would be there on top, looking down on everything. He could hardly wait.

The great day finally arrived and the man, who was now old, walked the last few steps up the slope to the very top. "Aha!" he thought, "How many people have looked up to this mountain and never reached it? But I, after months and years of constant effort, have finally reached my goal."

Just at that moment, he noticed a little boy. What was he doing there? How had he gotten there?

He could not believe his eyes! He had labored for years, many more years than this boy had even lived on earth, to reach the mountain top. How could the boy have gotten there first?

He stood there with his mouth hanging open in amazement. When he finally recovered his senses, he asked the child, "How did you get here? It took me many years of steady climbing. How did you come?"

The little boy replied simply, "You began at the bottom of the mountain and had to cover all the distance up to the top; I was born here."

The chasid had finished the parable and addressed his audience. "We all agree that the Sefas Emes is very young. No one denies that fact. But we must bear something else in mind. While others have achieved Torah greatness, scholarship, and piety by hard work over a lifetime, he was *born* to greatness, he was already on the peak when he came into the world. Small wonder then, that he is already fit to lead all his chasidim, young and old alike."

The Voices Burst Forth

וְהִנֵּה נַעַר בֹּכֶה... וַתֹּאמֶר מִיַּלְדֵי הָעִבְרִים זֶה

And lo, a lad was weeping...And she said: this one is from the children of the Hebrews (2:6)

From the very weeping of this one infant could be heard the cries of many Jewish babies.

(Writings)

"Something must be done about our situation! It is unbearable. We Jews are suffering to the limit of our endurance!"

"We can bear this no longer. Our people will be totally crushed unless something is done!"

This was a meeting of the leaders of the Jewish community of Prague. The Jews, beset by enemies at the royal court, were overtaxed and restricted in everything they did. But they knew who was behind all the harsh decrees.

"It is the queen's fault. We must send someone to speak to her and plead our cause. Perhaps if we approach Queen Maria Theresa directly, she will have pity on us."

"That is an excellent idea. Of course, the only candidate for such an important mission is Reb Zalman Karov, the wealthy financier. He has influence everywhere. He will be able to get an audience with the Queen. When he stands before her, he will plead our case capably. She will surely be impressed by him and convinced by his sincerity."

"Hear! Hear! That is the solution!" Cries arose from all those gathered at the emergency meeting. And so, it was unanimously decided to send Reb Zalman to speak to the Queen.

Without too much effort Reb Zalman secured an appointment with Her Royal Majesty. The day arrived. Reb Zalman went to the palace. He was ushered into the Queen's presence. As he stood before her, a loud cry suddenly escaped his throat. Everyone was horrified.

"Why did you cry out?" the Queen asked. "Don't you know that even your Torah teaches that the words of the wise are heard in calmness?"

Shaken himself by the sudden involuntary outburst, Reb Zalman explained, "Your Majesty, know that I do not stand here before you as an individual. I am representing my oppressed brethren. And when I opened my mouth to speak to you, their combined cry of suffering and pain suddenly burst forth from my throat. It was not my cry but their bitterness welling up and expressing itself."

Ten Men but No Minyan

לָמָּה תַכֶּה רֵעֶךָ

Why do you strike your fellow Jew? (2:13)

It was the day of the Rebbe's *yahrtzeit* for his mother. R' Yitzchak Meir, the first Gerrer Rebbe, or the Chidushei Harim, as he was also known, wished to pray with a *minyan* of ten in his own home, and had asked a young chasid to gather a group to go to his study for the morning prayer.

What a privilege to be asked to pray together with the Rebbe! A rare honor! Men vied to be part of the select group, but in a short time the young man who had already prayed had singled out ten men who would form the *minyan*. It was no surprise, though, that another man pushed himself forward to join the group and enter the Rebbe's room.

"The Rebbe said that he only wanted ten men. There is no room for you!" the young man said, turning him away from the door. The eleventh man was so disappointed that in his frustration, he tried to force his way in. The organizer lost his wits and slapped him across the face. The eleventh man, deeply insulted, turned away and stalked out of the building.

At *minchah* time the Rebbe again went to the young man and asked him to gather a group of ten to make a *minyan*. Since the young man had not yet prayed himself, he gathered nine men and included himself as the tenth.

When the group was rounded up, he led them into the Rebbe's room.

The Rebbe studied the group with his piercing look, then said, "I think that there is one missing."

The young man made a quick count and saw that there were ten men, aside from the Rebbe. "There is a *minyan* here," he assured the Rebbe.

"You must have included yourself in the number, then," the Chidushei Harim noted. The young man nodded, raising his eyebrows in question. The Rebbe explained,

"I don't see how we can include you in a *minyan*. Did you not lift your hand against a Jew today?"

The Symphony of Tears

וַיִּשְׁמַע אֱ-לֹקִים אֶת נַאֲקָתָם
And Hashem heard their groaning (2:24)

R' Shmuel Mohliver was once visiting Carlsbad. At that time the city was split by a raging controversy. There were some in the community who wished to bring an organ into the synagogue to replace the "old-fashioned" *chazzan*. Thinking that the visiting rabbi was a modern man who approved of their ideas, the Reform faction came to him and asked him to use his influence to get the organ accepted.

In answer, R' Shmuel told the following true story which had taken place in Bialystock.

A fire once broke out in the city, destroying the entire property of a certain wealthy Jew. He was left destitute without even a roof over his head. This rich man had a brother who was exceptionally gifted with musical talent though not with any common sense or tact. When he came to visit his brother right after the fire, he found the entire family sitting in the ruins of their home, weeping and wailing.

"What beautiful voices you have!" he said, his ears attuned to the sound they were making as they cried and moaned. "If you only sobbed together in rhythm, you could produce great music. Wait! I know! I will assign you parts: tenor, bass, alto. And when I give the signal, all begin at once and weep in time to my baton."

R' Shmuel turned to the Reform faction and said, "You are just like that foolish brother. A Jew comes to the synagogue in order to pour out his heart to His Creator and express his woes. And you come along and wish to orchestrate his pleading?! You wish to make him pray in tune and with rhythm."

I Also Scream!

כִּי יָדַעְתִּי אֶת מַכְאֹבָיו

For I know their pains (3:7)

Hashem alone knew of their suffering, for the Jews did not complain. In the merit of their silence they were indeed liberated.

(Holy works)

R' Yisrael of Modzitz, the famous Rebbe whose music became legend throughout chasidic circles, was once very ill. He was taken to a Berlin hospital for surgery and lay there in a room, afterwards, slowly recovering. One day the surgeon who was treating him entered the room and rubbing his hands with satisfaction, said, "Good morning, honored rabbi! I have just come from the bedside of another patient of mine, lying here in the hospital. I happened to mention you in high praise, comparing your behavior to his. He is a government minister who has just undergone surgery less difficult and painful than yours. Yet he lies there moaning and screaming with pain. I told him that you must be suffering even more than he, yet we do not hear a peep out of you. On the contrary, you continue to sing and compose beautiful tunes. I told him to use you as an example of how one should overcome pain."

"Herr Doktor," the Rebbe said as he lay helplessly on his back. "do not think that since I do not scream and writhe with pain, I am not also suffering. But, when I open my mouth to shout, I do not let the sounds emerge as screams of pain. I do not want to utter any sound in vain, therefore, the sound I make emerges as music and song in praise to my G-d."

There is Gold Here Too!

אֶרֶץ טוֹבָה וּרְחָבָה

A good and spacious land (3:8)

One of the many disciples of R' Shimon bar Yochai once left *Eretz Yisrael* to make his fortune abroad. He engaged in business and was very successful, returning to his homeland after several years, a very wealthy man.

His colleagues, who had remained behind and studied diligently all this time, could not help being jealous of their friend's success. They struggled for their very existence, subsisting on bread and water, living a life of hardship. If they could only do the same — go abroad and earn a tidy sum of money — they could continue their studies in comfort for the rest of their days!

R' Shimon, who sensed their jealousy, wished to burst the bubble of their wishful thinking. Gathering them together, he led them to a large valley near Meron.

As they stood there on a mountain slope, he turned to the valley below and prayed, "Valley, valley! Fill up with golden *dinarim*!"

Suddenly, right before their very eyes, the valley began filling up with gleaming coins of pure gold, thousands, millions of coins.

R' Shimon looked at the wonder in his *talmidim*'s eyes and said, "Is it gold that you desire? Then there is no need for you to travel abroad, to labor and exert yourselves. Here, before you, is a valley full of gold. Whosoever wishes to do so can go down and take to his heart's content. Go! Go ahead and gather up the coins!"

"But," R' Shimon continued, "you must keep one thing in mind, whatever you take now is deducted from your account in heaven. Torah study is not rewarded here on earth but in the World-to-Come."

No one made a move to go down and gather up the gold. For the rest of their lives they were content to remain in *Eretz Yisrael*, by their Rebbe's side, and continue studying Torah. Wealth and gold no longer had any appeal for them.

(According to *Midrash Shemos Rabbah*, Chapter 52)

The Love for Torah

מִי שָׂם פֶּה לָאָדָם

Who gave man a mouth (4:11)

Two brothers who had been born dumb, were neighbors of R' Yehudah Hanasi. They were unable to speak, but they were not deaf. They could hear and understand everything even though they could not communicate in speech. Since they very much desired to study Torah, they resolved that nothing would stand in their way. They would go to R' Yehudah's *beis midrash* and absorb all the knowledge that they could, even though they were handicapped.

Each morning, when they saw Rebbi (as he was also called) going to the *yeshivah*, they would hurry behind him so as not to miss one precious word. They sat among the other students and listened carefully. They would nod their heads and move their lips, but they could not add comments or ask questions.

R' Yehudah could not help noticing their devotion to Torah. His heart went out to these two brothers who could not express themselves and he prayed to *Hashem* to cure them.

Hashem heard the prayer of this great man and answered it! One morning when the brothers arrived at the *beis midrash*, they opened their mouths and suddenly found that they could speak!

The entire gathering rejoiced together with the brothers. They began talking to them and to their amazement, saw that these two were great scholars. They had absorbed a wealth of Torah knowledge over the years from R' Yehudah's lessons and had not forgotten a thing!

(Adapted from Tractate *Chagigah 3b*)

The Stutterer

לֹא עַתָּה יֵבוֹשׁ יַעֲקֹב וְלֹא עַתָּה פָּנָיו יֶחֱוָרוּ

No longer will Yaakov be ashamed nor will his face pale

(Haftorah Parashas Shemos, Yeshayahu 29)

R' Nosson Tzvi Finkel, the famous *Mashgiach* of Slobodka, once surprised the people in the synagogue by stuttering during *Kaddish*. He had asked to lead the *minchah* prayers but when he came to the *Kaddish*, he said it as if he were totally unfamiliar with the Aramaic words. People could not stop talking about it.

After some investigation, the whole story came to light. In this particular synagogue there was a mourner who led the *davening*. He was an unlearned man who was even unfamiliar with the *siddur* and often stumbled over words. Each time that he made a mistake, people would snicker and chuckle.

R' Nosson Tzvi Finkel had learned about this and resolved to correct it. He had decided to lead the prayers in that synagogue, while the mourner was present and show that anyone, even a learned man, can make a mistake in pronunciation. The mourner — thought R' Nosson Tzvi — would not feel so badly the next time he stumbled over the words.

The Secret of the Cholent

לֹא עַתָּה יֵבוֹשׁ יַעֲקֹב וְלֹא עַתָּה פָּנָיו יֶחֱוָרוּ
No longer will Yaakov be ashamed nor will his face pale
(Haftorah Parashas Shemos, Yeshayahu 29)

R' Avigdor Halberstam, the *av beis din* of Dokla, once spent a *Shabbos* in a small town and was invited to stay at the home of one of its prominent members.

It was the custom in those days that the guest was honored with the serving of the hot *cholent* on *Shabbos* morning after prayer. The *cholent,* with its juicy potatoes and meaty bones, was brought in and placed, according to the custom, before the distinguished guest, R' Avigdor.

The steam rose to R' Avigdor's nose and he dipped the ladle into the *cholent,* scooping out a portion onto his plate. Everyone waited eagerly to receive their portions but to their surprise, R' Avigdor began eating and continued eating until he had finished his portion. Everyone expected to be served now. But no! R' Avigdor took another portion and began eating that too! No one dared say a word. All eyes were fixed upon the visitor as he ate spoonful after spoonful, and plateful after plateful. Soon he had finished the entire *cholent* and no one had received as much as a bean!

They thought that he was finished at last. But no! R' Avigdor asked his hostess if there was any more *cholent* in the pot! Wordlessly, she went back into the kitchen and returned with the rest of the stew in the pot. R' Avigdor ate all that up too! There was no *cholent* for the family that week.

No one asked him any questions. They thought that R' Avigdor certainly must have had deep *kavanos* when he ate that *Shabbos cholent*.

It took a long time for the mystery to be cleared up. R' Avigdor himself revealed the secret a long time later. As soon as the steaming *cholent* had been placed before him, R' Avigdor had smelled something odd. When he had taken the first bite he saw that his sense of smell had not deceived him. Instead of putting oil into the pot, the cook had inadvertently used kerosene.

"I did not want the family to find out, for they would have surely have been angry at the poor cook and they might have dismissed her," said R' Avigdor. "I had pity on her. I decided that I preferred my hosts to think that I was a glutton rather than have them punish the cook for her mistake. And so I ate up the entire *cholent* pot."

These, then, had been his profound thoughts while eating the *cholent*.

Giving Up One's Portion

בִּרְאֹתוֹ יְלָדָיו... יַקְדִּישׁוּ שְׁמִי

When he sees his children... that they sanctify My Name
(Haftorah Parashas Shemos, Yeshayahu 29)

About one hundred years ago the Russian government passed what was known as the dreaded *Cantonist decree.*

Young Jewish children were kidnapped from their fathers' homes and mothers' arms and drafted into the Czar's army for tens of years — and sometimes for their entire lives.

The army authorities tried to uproot Jewish practices and feelings from their young forced recruits. Small wonder that the youngsters most often left Judaism completely.

The bereft parents knew that they would never see their kidnapped son again. The child was taken from them forever. He was lost to them and to all of Israel.

Our story takes place in Kobrin which is part of the Volhin district. One day a group of Cantonists stormed into town to capture Jewish children. The cry spread quickly and people barricaded themselves in their homes. But the Cantonists succeeded in seizing two victims.

Sender, the tailor's son, and Srulik, the *shochet*'s son, eleven and twelve years old respectively, had gone for a swim in the river that fateful morning, for it was at the peak of summer. As they reached the river bank, they were suddenly ambushed, tied up with stout rope and thrown into a wagon by the Cantonists. Their cries for help were drowned out by the roaring of the river. They were whisked away as the Cantonists swept onward, looking for their next victims at the next town.

Sender whispered to his friend, "We have been kidnapped by the dreaded Cantonists."

"I know," Srulik whispered back. "What is going to become of us now, I wonder? Oh, our poor parents!"

"Poor us!" Sender, the younger, wept, tears streaming down his cheeks.

"Hush!" said Srulik, the older and more mature of the two. "Look at the good side of things. At least we are here together. We must strengthen one another and not succumb to discouragement and despair. If we trust in *Hashem,* we may be saved! We may still return home some day! Perhaps *Hashem* will perform some miracle for us!"

"You back there, keep quiet or you'll feel the whip," a gruff voice snarled at them.

The children fell silent. It was a long journey and towards evening the wagon finally stopped in a small village near the Volga River. They had reached their destination — a farm belonging to a Russian peasant called Petrov.

Their captors hauled them out of the wagon and stood them before the rough farmer. "See these two fellows?" said one of the kidnappers. "They are going to be your farm hands. We want you to train them and get them accustomed to hard work. Develop their muscles. Don't be soft on them. They are army material. You must make soldiers out of them."

He drew Petrov aside and added in a whisper, "Make certain that they forget all their Jewish nonsense. Make good Christians out of them too; that is just as important."

Thus began a new life for Sender and Srulik. It was not an easy one, for Petrov worked them hard. But the two boys soon caught on to even the most difficult chores and did them well.

Petrov was satisfied. But, no matter how he tried, he could not make them forget their Jewishness. The boys were staunch and steadfast.

"Why don't you eat your meat? It will make strong men out of you," he would urge them, seeing that they had left their plates untouched.

"We must not!" they would exclaim emphatically. "It is *treife*, forbidden to us."

No matter how he tried, he could not get them to touch the meat.

When it came to *Shabbos* observance, they were also firm. Petrov would demand, "Why do you refuse to work today?" They would remain motionless. Even when he beat them, they would not budge. He cursed them and flogged them with his leather whip, shouting, "Laggards! Lazy bones! Get up!" But nothing would help.

"It is *Shabbos* today," they would answer. "We must not do any work."

Petrov tried all kinds of approaches. When he saw that the whip did not work, he would speak to them softly. Nothing helped. The two boys proved stronger than he when it came to their religion. They were determined to remain Jews!

Their life was a harsh and bitter one yet they clung fiercely to the little that they had managed to absorb in their short lifetimes in their Jewish homes and at *cheder*.

They remained in the farmer's home for two years yet

did not swerve from their practices. Seeing that he had not changed their religious outlook, Petrov decided to go to the army headquarters in the capital and report his helplessness. He had been saddled with these obstinate boys long enough!

When he came to headquarters, he stated his name and said that he had business with the commander. He was soon ushered in. When he stood before the officer behind the desk he lowered his head in shame and confessed, "I have had much success in hardening their bodies and muscles. The two boys who were placed in my custody will make fine soldiers. But, they are as Jewish as they were when they came to me. They have not forgotten one single thing. They are stubborn, just like their people. I whipped them black and blue but could not get them to eat my meat or work when it did not suit them."

"What do you want? What do you suggest? How can we break their spirits?" the commander asked the peasant.

"I am at my wit's end. I have no suggestions. I have come here because I am sick and tired of having them slinking around my house with their prayer murmurings and stubborn habits. Obstinate creatures! I want them removed at once!"

The commander was thoughtful for a few minutes. Suddenly he thought of a drastic measure that would force the boys to abandon their Jewishness. He would baptize them by force! "Tomorrow I will send some soldiers to take them to the church. Once the priest sprinkles some of his holy water on them, they will no longer resist our teachings. At any rate, after tomorrow, they will no longer be in your hands so you need not worry."

Petrov sighed with relief and left the office. He returned to his home in the village feeling as if a heavy load had been removed from his shoulders. He had not realized what a burden the boys had been.

As soon as he drove into his front yard he found Sender splitting logs. He was cutting a double amount since it was Friday and on Saturday he never worked.

"Where is your friend, Srulik?" the peasant asked.

"He is in the fields, working," Sender replied curtly.

"Hmmm," said the farmer. "I really wanted to tell you the news together but it does't matter. You can tell him yourself. Tomorrow is the big day! Ah! Tomorrow!"

Sender opened his eyes wide. What did Petrov mean? Petrov could not contain his excitement and revealed the secret. "I wanted to make good Christians out of you! I was determined to succeed but you two were stronger than I. Still, I have not failed altogether. What I was unable to do with kindness, the Church and the army will do by force. Tomorrow the army is sending some soldiers to seize you and take you to church. Do you know what they will do to you there?" he asked with a gleam in his eye.

Sender caught his breath. He did not answer but Petrov really did not expect any answer. He supplied it gladly himself. "There, in church, you will be properly baptized, against your will! Nothing will stop us from succeeding!" he said with elation and chuckling merrily, he turned and went inside the house.

Sender was left standing, stunned and shocked. But in a flash he was running to Srulik, in the field. "Srulik! Srulik!" he shouted hysterically, tears streaming down his cheeks.

"What is the matter?" his friend asked in deep concern.

"What has happened?" Sender blurted the information out. When he had finished, he stood there, waiting for Srulik's reaction. Srulik was as dumbstruck as he had been. The two stood there in silence, not knowing what to do or what to say. And yet the entire air around them seemed to ask, "What now?"

Tearfully, they raised their eyes towards heaven, hoping that their help would come from on high. Suddenly Sender jumped up. "I have it! I know!" he exulted.

Srulik's eyes lit up with hope but when Sender began unfolding his drastic plan, they dimmed.

"Tomorrow," said Sender, "when the soldiers come to fetch us, they will have to travel over the bridge that spans the deep river below. When we reach that spot we will have to make a supreme effort to break away and jump. We will throw ourselves into the river! We must die rather than let ourselves be converted! It is the only way!"

Srulik's face stiffened. Grimly, he replied, "We will be saved from conversion. That is true. But we will not escape being punished in *gehinnom.* I remember learning from my father that whoever commits suicide is denied any portion in the World-to-Come."

The two stood there. Finally Sender said, "No matter! Despite that terrible punishment, I refuse to allow myself to be converted! I had rather lose my portion in *olam haba* than be converted and live as a Christian. I will make that sacrifice!"

Srulik agreed with him. "You are right, Sender'l. It is worth it. We will follow your plan."

Determined to carry out the suicide pact, they returned to their room to make their preparations. It was already night. The boys lay on their beds, unable to fall asleep. "It is our very last night here, our last night on earth. How can we waste it in idle sleep?" they asked one another. And so they lay there, whispering to each other, waiting until all signs of activity stopped. They heard Petrov stomping up the stairs to his bedroom. Soon he was snoring soundly.

Stealthily, they arose and began stripping the walls of all the crucifixes and pictures of Christian 'saints' with which Petrov had filled the room in his hope to convert them. Silently they lifted the window sash and began throwing all of these things outside into the bushes. They made no sound in falling. Soon the room was purified. The boys now burst into fervent prayer, pleading, "O *Hashem*! Save us!" They begged for their lives, wept for their souls. They were so absorbed in their prayer that they did not even hear the sound of wagon wheels and hoofbeats coming up the road.

A wagon approached and stopped right in Petrov's driveway. Two men leaped out and began shouting, "Hey, Petrov! Where are you? Get out of bed and let us in!"

The boys were wrenched from their prayers and brought back down to earth. They rushed to their beds and pretended that they were asleep.

After a few minutes of pounding on the front door, the two men were rewarded with an answer from Petrov. He stuck his head out of the bedroom window, asking, "Who is that downstairs? Who is waking a decent farmer up at this unearthly hour of night? What do you want, down there?"

"We want you, Petrov. Get dressed. Come down and open up."

Petrov jumped into his trousers and ran down. He

opened the front door but did not recognize the two burly soldiers who stood there. "What do you want of me at this time of night?" he asked in alarm.

"Aha! So you are the treacherous Petrov! You revealed the army's plan to your two Jewish charges, didn't you? You cannot deny it because we have our spies and our ways of finding out things. We learned that your two boys have been planning an escape and were sent here before they could get away."

"That's right!" said the second soldier. "We have come to seize the birds before they fly the coop. We are smarter than they; we are always one step ahead and have come in the middle of the night. We are going to tie them up and take them straight to the city where they will be ripe and ready for an early baptism!"

The two men brushed the confused Petrov aside and stormed up the steps. They found the boys' room and the two victims lying safe in bed. They gloated, "The birds are still safe in their cage. They have not escaped yet and now they will surely not escape their fate."

Sender and Srulik tried to squirm as the two men trussed them up like chickens for slaughter. They shivered at the look of these burly, coarse men who handled them so roughly. The men slung the two bodies over their shoulders like two sacks of potatoes, skipped down the stairs and threw them into the back of the wagon. One of them climbed into the driver's seat and the other went into the back, together with the boys. Soon the wagon was on its way.

Sender tried to roll over close to Srulik so that he could whisper in his ear. "Soon we will be crossing over the bridge. Let us pray to *Hashem* that He give us strength for one sudden spurt, enough to leap out of the wagon and roll off the bridge, even though we are tied up. This is it! Be strong, Srulik! We must make it!"

"Alright! I am ready. Be strong, too, Sender. Good luck!"

"*Amen*! And to you too!" Srulik replied.

The two boys had been whispering in Yiddish, hoping that even if the soldiers heard, they would not understand.

But to their surprise, as soon as the words were out of their mouth, one of the soldiers, a heavyset, frightening brute of a man, put his two meaty hands on the boys. They felt like heavy weights. They boys were trapped underneath those paws, unable to budge.

"He must understand Yiddish!" Srulik thought, not daring to voice this guess.

Sender wept silently, not daring to raise his voice.

After a few minutes of lying very still, the boys tried to squirm to the right or the left but they were held in a tight vise-like grip.

The wagon rolled noisily over the wooden bridge and continued on beyond. Their plan was foiled. There was nothing that they could do now. The vehicle rolled on until it reached a crossroads. But instead of taking the fork that led to the city where army headquarters were and where the Church was waiting to convert them, it took the other fork, leading to a different city!

What was going on? The wagon sped on for a while and suddenly came to a halt. The two soldiers approached the boys with open knives in their hands. "This is the end!" they thought, prepared for the worst. But no, instead of going for their throats, the soldiers began cutting their ropes. Soon the boys were free to move their hands and feet. They sat up, rubbing their eyes in bewilderment.

"What is going on here?" Sender ventured to express his astonishment.

"Aren't you Cossacks? Soldiers in the Czar's army?" Srulik asked, also voicing his surprise.

They were amazed at how gentle the soldier's voices sounded now. One said, "We were Cossacks until recently. Like you, we were also kidnapped into the Russian army, many years ago. Over the years we lost all traces of our Jewishness. But, when we learned of your courage and bravery, when we heard how you stood up to Petrov the *goy* over two years of hardship and beatings, our hearts went out to you and we felt ashamed. We decided to return to Judaism and our first act of loyalty would be to rescue you two from baptism and death."

Tears of joy slipped down the boys' cheeks. Srulik turned to his friend and smiled through his tears, "What did I tell you? *Hashem*'s salvation comes in the twinking of an eye!"

The wagon with its four occupants traveled all through that night, stopping towards morning in a small town where Srulik's uncle served as rabbi. The two boys were taken to his home.

After an emotional reunion, Srulik sketched the events of the past two years, dwelling upon his miraculous escape. Pointing to his friend, he said, "It is only thanks to Sender that we were saved from conversion for he was prepared to forego his portion in *olam haba* by committing suicide rather than undergo baptism! He is the real hero here!"

Sender blushed and looked down at the table but

Srulik's uncle, the rabbi, spoke to him and made him look up, "Blessed are you, my dear boy! Such a pure intention and thought is dearer to *Hashem* than all of the World-to-Come!"

Who is to Be Pitied?

כִּי בִרְאוֹתוֹ יְלָדָיו... אֱלֹקֵי יִשְׂרָאֵל יַעֲרִיצוּ

When he sees his children... they shall stand in awe of the G-d of Israel

(Haftorah Parashas Shemos, Yeshayah 29:23)

The ship sailed along, carrying many passengers from different countries. All of them were heathen, idol worshippers, except for one small Jewish lad who was traveling all alone. He was on his way home to *Eretz Yisrael*. He sat among the other passengers feeling very lonely.

They sailed calmly on the tranquil blue waters when suddenly, the waters turned an angry grey and foamed and crashed against the ship, tossing it to and fro. The waves washed over the deck and into the hold, threatening to sink them.

The passengers were panic-stricken. They prayed to their idols but nothing happened. The waves continued pounding against the side of the ship.

Even the sailors were frightened. Never had they experienced such a fierce storm. They looked around and noticed the Jewish boy, the only one who was not praying.

"Look at him! Why doesn't he pray like us?" they asked.

"Why don't you pray like us?" people asked him. "You are a Jewish boy. You have a mighty G-d Who hears the prayers of His people and answers them! Perhaps He will perform a miracle for you, if you ask for it. Pray! Your life is at stake!"

The boy lifted his voice in prayer. "*Hashem*! A-mighty G-d! Please save me. Stop this fearful storm! Command the winds to subside and the sea to become calm, so that I can reach my home safely. I know that all the idols to which the other passengers pray are helpless and worthless. Only You can save this ship, *Hashem*! Show Your great might and help us!"

Hashem, indeed, heard the boy's prayer. He calmed the sea and scattered the winds and clouds. Soon it was peaceful again and the ship resumed its course.

The ship docked at a port before reaching *Eretz Yisrael*. Many of the passengers were happy for an opportunity to get off onto dry land and purchase fresh food. They asked the boy to come along and enjoy the stopover. "You can buy some fresh fruits, too. It will be a nice change from your regular food."

"But I am not familiar with the city," he said. "I don't know the language and do not know my way around. I would not know where to buy anything... I am all alone and helpless."

"You, pitiful and helpless?" the people laughed. "How strange! We are the ones who should feel alone and helpless. Our idols of gold and silver were unable to help us. We are the helpless ones! You are fortunate. You are protected and safe, for, wherever you are, you always have the A-mighty by your side. Even if you think that you are alone, your G-d is always there to protect you from any harm!"

(According to *Yerushalmi, Berachos, Perek 9 Halachah 1*)

The Butcher's Secret

וּבְטֶרֶם תֵּצֵא מֵרֶחֶם הִקְדַּשְׁתִּיךָ
"Before you emerged from the womb did I sanctify you"
(Haftorah Parashas Shemos, Yirmiyah 1)

In his youth, R' Meir of Premislan studied under the saintly R' Dov of Podhitz. Every Thursday, the market day in Podhitz, the ten-year-old boy would go out among the many vendors and gather pennies for charity. He would distribute his collection among the many poor who did not have the means to buy food for *Shabbos*.

One time, when the young boy approached Shimon the butcher for his usual donation, Shimon said, "Meir'l, I'll make a deal with you. I will give you four *zuz* provided that you tell me if the bull which I want to buy is kosher or not."

The boy was not surprised by this request. Full of

confidence he said, "I will tell you — but only for five *zuz*!"

The butcher thought for a while and decided to gamble. Taking out five *zuz*, he gave it to the boy and then pointed out the animal he was considering buying. Meir'l looked at the animal and immediately said, "It is *treife*. That is not a kosher animal."

The butcher needed a kosher animal for meat. He turned to the likeable lad once again, and pointing to another steer asked, "How about that one? Is that kosher?"

Meir'l had his wits about him and said, "I'll tell you, but only for another five *zuz*."

The butcher handed him another five *zuz* and the boy gave his verdict, "That animal is kosher. It is *kosher lemehadrin*!"

Meir'l was not a common child. Besides, all the money he received went straight to the poor. Yet, the butcher was not entirely certain that his predictions were accurate. He was eager to test the accuracy of Meir'l's statements and decided to buy both animals!

Just as Meir had said, the first animal proved to be *treife* and the second, *glatt*, everything in order.

A week passed and it was again market day in Podhitz. Meir'l came along as usual to make the rounds so that poor families would have food that *Shabbos*. When Shimon the butcher saw him, he called the lad over and offered him a deal; "I'll give you twenty *zuz* for your services today. I want you to tell me which of the animals I intend to buy will be kosher and which not."

"I want five *zuz* for *each* animal," Meir'l insisted.

Shimon agreed. He took out his wallet and began

making the rounds with Meir'l, pointing out an animal and asking him for his opinion, paying the fee for each answer. Meir would say, "kosher," and the butcher would buy. Meir would say, "*treife*," and the butcher would not buy.

Meir'l did very well that day and was overjoyed. Now he could be generous to the poor people who depended upon him for the food on their *Shabbos* table. And there was another advantage; he would not have to take as much time away from his studies for this act of charity.

From then on, he and Shimon worked together, both partners satisfied with their deal. Shimon began prospering because he never bought a *treife* animal. He had no losses! All of his animals were kosher. Pure profit. People could not understand why he was becoming richer and richer while the other butchers of Podhitz were getting poorer and poorer.

The disgruntled butchers finally got together and went to the rabbi, R' Dov. They complained of favoritism; they claimed that the *shochtim* were arbitrarily ruling all of Shimon's animals as kosher and all of theirs as *treife*. The *shochtim* were summoned to defend their honor. Were they really slanting the *halachah* to help one man and harm another? The slaughterers, of course, said that they performed their duties honestly. Was it their fault that all of Shimon's animals happened to be kosher, or the others happened to be *treife*? That was how things turned out.

No one understood the secret of Shimon's success. Something lay behind his infallible judgment in buying cattle. The butchers decided to check on his movements to see if they could discover anything unusual.

They waited for the following Thursday, then watched

him carefully. They saw Shimon walking around the cattle pens accompanied by a small boy, Meir'l. Shimon would point out an animal, and Meir would say something. Then he would pay the boy five *zuz*. This happened time after time until Shimon had picked out the animals that he intended to buy. When the two had parted, the butchers called Meir'l over and begged, "Meir'l, please pray for us, too, just like you pray for Shimon."

He looked up at them in innocent surprise. "But I don't pray for Shimon," he said.

"Well, then, do for us whatever you do for him! Please!" they begged.

"But I really don't do anything for him. If he asks me if a certain animal is kosher, I tell him yes or no and he pays me five *zuz* each time. That is all. I am willing to do the same for you. For the same fee, of course."

The butchers eagerly handed him their money and asked their questions, pointing to one steer after another. Each time Meir would tell them if the animal was kosher or not, just as he had done for Shimon. They were very, very satisfied. But, they also learned that they could not strike bargains with him. It was the full fee for each animal, five *zuz*, no package deals.

This might have gone on indefinitely, with all of the butchers of Podhitz getting rich, thanks to young Meir'l's prophetic talents. But the matter came to the attention of R' Dov, the boy's teacher, and he put a stop to it. He scolded his student for using his holy talents and forbade him from saying anything that would indicate that he was blessed with divine intuition.

The King's Strange Dream

הִפְקַדְתִּיךָ הַיּוֹם הַזֶּה עַל הַגּוֹיִם וְעַל הַמַּמְלָכוֹת לִנְתוֹשׁ
וְלִנְתוֹץ... לִבְנוֹת וְלִנְטוֹעַ

"I have assigned you this day over the nations and over the kingdoms to root out and to pull down... to build and to plant"
(Haftorah Parashas Shemos, Yirmiyah 1)

R' Yehudah Leib ben Bezalel, the Maharal of Prague, creator of the Golem, was a trusted and honored advisor to his king, Rudolf the Second. Because he was a Jew and because he was held in such trust and honor, R' Yehudah Leib was hated by several of the king's ministers. They envied him his position and plotted to have him and the entire Jewish community banished from Prague. They knew that the king would not, on his own, agree to drive the Jews out. And so, they decided to enlist the help of his queen. She fell in with their plans.

One evening, when King Rudolf retired to his chambers after a busy day, she waved a piece of paper before him and asked him to sign. "This is a decree banishing the Jews," she said. "Your ministers have worked out everything down to the smallest detail. It only lacks your signature to be put into law." The king did not want to be rushed into something so decisive and pushed the paper aside. But, when the queen coaxed him again and again, he finally told her that he would put the document under his pillow and think the matter over that night. He would give his answer in the morning.

The queen knew not to press him any more. True to his word, Rudolf put the paper under his pillow. But he did not give the matter any thought; he slept soundly, without a care. Towards morning he began dreaming.

He found himself in a bitter battle. He was defeated and captured. His captors exiled him to their land and threw him into a prison tower to rot until he died. He languished there for years and years, tormented by the glimpses of the outside world which he could see from the tiny barred window in his cell.

The king spent most of his days with his nose pressed against his tiny window. One day he noticed a bearded figure, a Jew, standing in front of the tower, looking up at his window. The king beckoned to him and then said,

"I am King Rudolf. Don't you recognize me?"

The bearded man shook his head. "You don't look like King Rudolf."

"But I am the king, nevertheless. Believe me! I am ready to swear to it! Please, can you free me from this prison?" he pleaded.

The old man raised the stick in his hand and struck the stone wall. To the king's amazement, it split. He was free! He gazed around him, blinking in the sunlight, too happy to speak.

The old man took the king's hand and spoke to him gently, "Your Majesty," said the old Jew, "come with me to my house. I will have a tailor fit you with a new set of clothing and a barber trim your hair and beard so that you look presentable. You must rest up and regain your strength before you return home to your kingdom. You, certainly, cannot go back looking as you do now!"

The king felt the dream receding and he suddenly awoke. What a nightmare! There was only one person who would be able to explain that strange dream to him.

The man who resembled the old Jew in his dream, R' Yehudah Leib. The king sent for him at once, even though it was still early in the morning.

The Maharal came to the palace and was led right into the king's bedroom. As soon as he saw him, the king greeted the rabbi, told him of the dream, and asked, "Why did you not recognize me at first in the dream?"

The Maharal answered with dignity, "Because Your Majesty was so changed, so different."

"What do you mean by that?" King Rudolf asked.

The Maharal replied, "When you went to bed last night, your head was filled with strange, evil thoughts, hostile to me, your good friend, and to your devoted subjects, the Jews. What did you put under your pillow to give you such terrible thoughts?"

Suddenly the king recalled the document regarding the banishment of the entire Jewish community from Prague. He withdrew the piece of paper and tore it up before the Maharal, vowing, "Never, for the rest of my life, will I pass any decree harmful to your people!"

The Maharal's expression softened and he said, "*Hashem* will truly reward you, for our G-d punishes and rewards with an exact measure. Since you promised never to harm the Jews, He will protect and preserve you too, as you saw in the dream. It was to have come true, but your worthy deed, just now, and your promise will prevent the nightmare from becoming reality. *Hashem* will continue to protect you too, as long as you keep your promise."

Throughout his lifetime, Rudolf the Second reigned supreme and the Jews under his rule enjoyed his favor and protection.

פָּרָשַׁת וָאֵרָא

Parashas Va'eyra

The Wonderful Treasure

וַיֹּאמֶר אֵלָיו אֲנִי ה׳

And he said to him: I am Hashem (6:2)

I am Hashem — trustworthy to pay reward.
(Rashi)

This story takes place during the time of the *Beis Hamikdash*. The Jews were making their pilgrimage to Jerusalem for the festival of *Succos*, to rejoice before *Hashem* and to pray in the *Beis Hamikdash*.

That year had been a very dry one. Rain falls only during the winter in *Eretz Yisrael*, and the winter before had not been blessed with rains. The water cisterns had not been filled. Throughout the hot summer, people had hoarded every drop of water in their wells and cisterns very carefully. But, by now, there was hardly anything left. Rain had not yet fallen.

The pilgrims, the *olei regel*, were thirsty after their long journey in the hot sun. The old men and the young children, the donkeys which they had ridden and the animals which they had brought for their sacrifices — all these were very thirsty. But, there was no water.

A wealthy Jew named Nakdimon ben Gurion saw the plight of his people and wept. He longed to help them, to quench their thirst. But how?

Finally, he thought of a solution. He knew of a Roman officer who lived in Jerusalem and owned twelve fresh springs of water. These springs bubbled up from the ground, winter and summer, though less so in the summer. If only he could borrow these springs.

Nakdimon visited the Roman and explained his predicament. "If you allow me to have the use of those springs, I promise to return the water that the people drink."

"But how will you pay back the water?" the officer demanded.

Nakdimon replied, "It is autumn now. My people have come here to pray in our *Beis Hamikdash* for rain. We will pray harder than ever for plentiful rain to fall. This will replenish the underground sources and your fountains will bubble forth stronger than ever!"

"That is fine and well. But, what if it doesn't rain? What if we have a drought like last year? How can you guarantee my water?"

Nakdimon had an answer for this too. "If it does not rain within one month, I will pay you twelve talents of silver, one talent for each fountain."

This was a huge sum! Enough to sway the hardest of Roman officers. If rain did not fall, he would still have his springs and a tremendous fortune besides! "Very well. I accept your offer," the Roman said.

Nakdimon now led the thirsty travelers to the twelve springs and let them drink their fill from the fresh underground water. Refreshed, they were able to enjoy their festival to the utmost.

Succos was over and everyone returned home. Days and weeks passed and it was already well into autumn but there still was no rain! The skies were as blue as ever

with no trace of a raincloud. The land was parched. The water cisterns were bone dry. Even the fountains and springs were down to a bare trickle. There was no water to be had anywhere now.

What about Nakdimon's agreement? The day was fast approaching when he would have to produce rain or else pay the penalty. The Roman officer was not disturbed in the least. He preferred the money to the water. He would be rich!

On the morning of the appointed day the Roman officer sent a messenger to Nakdimon saying, "Today is the day. Water or money."

Nakdimon answered, "The day is still young. I have plenty of time!" He had not yet given up hope.

The morning passed. It was noon. The officer sent another reminder, demanding either water or money.

"It is only noon," Nakdimon said, firm in his faith that *Hashem* would come to his aid.

Towards evening, the messenger came for the third time, demanding immediate payment. Nakdimon noted that the sun had not yet set.

Certain that the money was already as good as in his treasury, the officer mocked, "If it has not rained until now, what makes you think that it will rain in the next hour? Surely not! Get your money ready."

The Roman sent out invitations to all his friends to come to a celebration that evening. He expected to be rich and wanted to share his good fortune with them. While his servants were busy with the preparations, he went to the bathhouse to bathe for the joyous event.

Nakdimon was very sad. What could he do? He went to the *Beis Hamikdash* and wrapped himself up in his *tallis*. Then he lifted his voice in prayer, "Master of the world!

Surely, You are aware that what I did, I did not do for my name or my family's honor. I did it for Your glory, so that the *olei regel* would be able to drink and rejoice properly on our festival, as You Yourself have commanded in the Torah. Without water, they would not have been happy; they would have suffered. But now, how am I to return the water that they drank to the Roman officer? How can I pay my obligation?"

As soon as he finished his prayer, the sky darkened. The clouds began to drop their heavy burden onto the ground. It rained. It poured. Soon all of the cisterns were filled and overflowing. The ground soaked up the rain greedily and the underground reservoirs were filled; the fountains gushed forth with plentiful water.

Just then the officer emerged from the bathhouse. Rain! He could not believe his eyes. Minutes ago, the sky had looked so blue. As he stood there, dumbfounded, Nakdimon came by, on his way back from the *Beis Hamikdash*. He found the officer wet, confused and angry.

Nakdimon greeted him, "Sir! You see that I have kept my bargain. I have returned all the water that I borrowed and much more! I really deserve change!"

The Roman turned on him angrily, "I know that your G-d did this for your sake. But your rejoicing is premature. You still owe me the money you promised, for the sun has already set. The rain that fell belongs to tomorrow and not to the day of our contract. You are late in keeping your promise and owe me the money."

It was dark outside. The Roman was right...

Discouraged, Nakdimon turned around and went back to the *Beis Hamikdash*. He again enveloped himself in his *tallis* and began to pray: "Master of the world! Show the entire world how You love Your people! Perform yet another miracle for them!"

A strong wind began to blow, scattering all of the clouds and revealing the sun behind them. It had not yet set; the day was not yet over. The Roman officer could no longer deny that Nakdimon had paid back his debt in full. He had no claim on the twelve silver talents for *Hashem* had performed another miracle.

(According to Tractate *Taanis 19b*)

The Reliable Guarantors

וַיֹּאמֶר אֵלָיו אֲנִי ה׳

And he said to him: I am Hashem (6:2)

I am Hashem — trustworthy to pay reward.
(Rashi)

Once the *yeshivah* of R' Akiva and his companions were in great financial straits. They could not supply the needs of their *talmidim*. They decided to borrow money from a wealthy Roman matron. R' Akiva, personally, went to ask for the loan.

He was ushered into her house with a gracious welcome. "Of what service could I be to you?" she asked. When R' Akiva presented his request, she agreed at once, even though the sum he mentioned was very large. But, she asked him if he could bring any guarantors to assure that the sum would be returned to her on time.

R' Akiva said, "You name any guarantor that you like."

"Very well," said the Roman matron. She thought, then replied, "I would like the guarantors to be *Hashem* and the sea. They shall make sure that I get my money back on time."

"Very well," said R' Akiva, gratefully accepting the loan.

Time passed and the date for returning the money had arrived. He had the money all ready to bring to the matron when he, suddenly, became ill and could not go.

The Roman matron stayed at home and waited for him to come. When morning had passed and he had not arrived, she went out to the terrace, stood by the sea and prayed, "Master of the world! Only You know why R' Akiva has not come to repay the debt. Whatever the reason, the money is missing and I need it. At the time that I lent him the money he promised that You and the sea would be the guarantors. Since he cannot come to fulfill his promise, I request that the guarantors make good the pledge. Please, send me back my money."

Hashem heard the good woman's prayer and answered it. Across the ocean in Rome, the royal princess was seized by a fit of madness. She gathered up all of her jewels and placed them in a chest. Clutching the chest, she ran to the shore and threw it far out to sea.

The sea was waiting to do *Hashem*'s bidding. It swept up the chest of gold and gems and carried it swiftly, all the way to the shores of *Eretz Yisrael*. The Roman matron was still waiting for her prayer to be answered when a huge wave came rushing towards her, bearing its treasure. It receded and the woman bent down to pick up the small chest. She took it into her house and opened it up. Its contents were worth far more than the sum she had lent to R' Akiva!

Some time passed and R' Akiva recovered from his illness. As soon as he was able to do so, he left his bed and rushed to pay back his debt. When he reached the matron's home he begged her not to be angry with him for the delay, explaining how ill he had been.

When he handed her the bag of money which he owed, she smiled and refused it, saying, "I cannot accept any money from you. Your debt was already paid back by the guarantors. In fact, I owe you money."

R' Akiva was puzzled. She went into the next room to fetch the small chest which the sea had thrown up at her feet. She gave R' Akiva the chest filled with gold. "This is what I owe you. The sea gave me much more than I originally lent you. This is for you and your needy disciples."

(Adapted from *Rashi* and the *Ran* on Tractate *Nedarim* 50a)

The Returned Loan

וַיֹּאמֶר אֵלָיו אֲנִי ה׳

And He said to him: I am Hashem (6:2)

I am Hashem — trustworthy to pay reward.
(Rashi)

There was a timid tap at R' Yeshaya's door. At his command, a man entered. R' Yeshaya did not know him. "Are you a stranger to Zochovitz?" he asked.

The man nodded. "Yes, I have just come recently and opened up a business. Rebbe, I need a loan of one thousand gold coins for half a year to keep me from going bankrupt. You are the only one I can turn to. Please help me."

The rabbi was thoughtful. "That is a large sum," he said. "I am quite willing to give it to you, but you must produce some person who can guarantee the loan, someone here in Zochovitz who knows you and will vouch for you."

Tears gathered in the man's eyes. "But no one knows me well enough. I don't know anyone who would give me a good reference and would sign for such a large loan. What shall I do? Only *Hashem* is a witness to my desperate situation and to my honesty. Only He would be able to guarantee this loan..." His voice trailed off weakly.

"You could have picked no better guarantor!" R' Yeshaya said and gave the man the entire sum he needed.

The half year passed. The date for the payment arrived and the man came to R' Yeshaya Zochovitzer to return the loan. This time he was beaming. "*Hashem* was very kind to me. The loan set me on my feet and put me in business. I have done very well this past year, thank G-d, and have come to pay back the thousand gold coins."

R' Yeshaya pushed away the money. "Your guarantor already paid me back."

"How can that be?" the borrower asked, thoroughly astonished.

R' Yeshaya nodded, "On the very day that I lent you the money, *Hashem* sent me an unusual business opportunity that netted me a profit of exactly one thousand coins! I canceled your debt because of that sum. You don't owe me anything!"

Why Be Boastful?

מִן הַמַּמְלָכוֹת תִּהְיֶה שְׁפָלָה וְלֹא תִתְנַשֵּׂא עוֹד

It shall be lowliest of the kingdoms, neither shall it ever lift itself up"

(Haftorah Parashas Va'eyra, Yechezkel 29)

A Jew once came to the Kotzker Rebbe with a personal request. "I suffer from pride. I would like to know how to rid myself of this undesirable trait," he said.

The Rebbe told him to be seated and wait.

The Rebbe's *shammash* showed in the next person. The Rebbe nodded to him and he sat down. "Rebbe, I have a daughter to marry off but I have no means. I am a poor man."

The Rebbe turned to the Jew sitting nearby and told him to give the poor man a generous donation to marry off his daughter.

"But Rebbe, I don't even have an extra penny for myself!" he wailed.

The Rebbe took care of that man and told his *shammash* to send the next person in. This time a Jew came in with a complex *halachic* problem. The Rebbe turned to the Jew who sat nearby and said, "Why don't you answer him?"

The Jew shrugged his shoulders helplessly. "But I never learned that. How can I give an answer?"

The Rebbe answered the question. Soon he was ready for the next person. This time a Jew entered asking the Rebbe for some business advice. The Rebbe turned again to the man sitting close at hand and said, "Perhaps you can give him some astute advice?"

The man shook his head, "I have no talent for business," he confessed.

The Rebbe dealt with him too and dismissed him. Then he turned to the overly proud man and said, "I do not understand. You have no money, no learning and no business acumen and still you boast. What, pray tell, do you have to boast about?!"

פָּרָשַׁת בֹּא

Parashas Bo

The Uninvited Sage

הַחֹדֶשׁ הַזֶּה לָכֶם רֹאשׁ חֳדָשִׁים

This month shall be to you the first of months (12:2)

When Hashem transmitted all the laws concerning the lunar calendar and its calculations to Moshe, He taught him how to determine the leap years and the months.

(Midrash)

Before the Jewish calendar, as we know it, was established for all generations, the New Moon was set month by month; leap years, year by year. One time, Rabban Gamliel saw the need to make a leap year. He invited seven Sages to come to him the next morning so that they could form a *beis din* for that purpose.

On the following morning, he found eight Sages waiting for him at the courtroom. He was upset and said, "Let the eighth one, who was not asked to come, leave at once."

Shmuel Hakatan rose and said, "I have come without invitation, but I did not come to sit in on the *beis din* to establish the leap year. I came to watch and learn."

Rabban Gamliel was mollified and said, "Sit down, my son. Really, you are worthy enough to determine all future leap years, but our Sages have already ruled that only those who have been asked can sit on such a *beis din*."

Shmuel Hakatan was in fact not the eighth one, who had not been invited. He *had* been asked to come, but in order to protect the man who had really not been invited and to spare him embarrassment, he had said that he was the one!

(According to Tractate *Sanhedrin 11a*)

The Last Request

הַחֹדֶשׁ הַזֶּה

This month... (12:2)

He showed him how the new moon looks.
(Rashi)

The merchant was faced with a difficult decision. He had been away since early that morning and longed to be home already, after a long day of business. It was dark now and he stood at a crossroads. One road led through a thick forest, a short cut that would bring him home two or three hours earlier. The other was longer. He hesitated at taking the shorter route; the forest was the known lair of thieves. And yet, he longed to be home already, seated comfortably in front of the hearth with a warm glass of tea cradled in his hands.

Home! Home! He tugged the reins to the right, to the

forest path. It was spooky and frightening, but he comforted himself with the thought of that glass of tea. Soon he would be home.

Suddenly, there was a burst of noise. Horses snorted and men whooped. Armed robbers surrounded the coach.

"What a find! What an excellent fish we have caught!" They shouted with glee at the sight of his fine carriage. The leader ordered his men to tie up the merchant. The robbers swarmed all over the carriage, pouncing upon everything they found inside. There were all kinds of food which he was bringing home from the big city for his family. They snatched at them and sat down to a large feast. They would take care of him later. But first — food!

After his men had gorged themselves, the leader turned to the victim. "It is an accepted custom that a man be given one last request before he dies. What do you want?"

"I don't want to die! I want to live!" the merchant sobbed.

"Don't be a fool! We cannot let you escape. Ask for something reasonable."

The Jew thought. Looking up at the heavens, he saw the new moon and suddenly remembered that he had not blessed it yet this month. "I would like to say a short prayer," he begged.

The leader agreed. He told his men to loosen the captive's bonds so that he might stand up and pray. The merchant prayed as he had never prayed before. He put all of his feelings into the words, the last *mitzvah* that he would be performing on earth. When he came to the phrase "Just as I dance before you but cannot touch you, so shall my enemies be unable to touch me to do me harm," he burst into heartrending sobs. He stood there, his cheeks wet with tears when, suddenly, a mighty wind began blowing. It lifted him up and away from the forest, to safety!

"Take the Scroll With You!"

הַחֹדֶשׁ הַזֶּה לָכֶם רֹאשׁ חֳדָשִׁים

This month shall be unto you the first of months (12:2)

The name Rothschild represents Jewish philanthropy. One of the Rothschilds, Baron Shimon Wolf Rothschild, was a truly devout, worthy Jew.

There was one commandment that Reb Shimon Wolf wished to observe in the best possible way. The Torah tells us that each person is required to write a *Sefer Torah*. Reb Shimon Wolf was determined to have his own Torah scroll. He did not rely on the local scribes of Germany. He felt that they were not well-versed enough in the intricate laws involved in writing a *Sefer Torah*. Instead he imported a *sofer* from Russia who enjoyed an excellent reputation as a master craftsman and a learned and holy Jew. The Baron commissioned him to write his personal *Sefer Torah* and he lodged with the Baron, Reb Shimon Wolf, during the months that it took to complete this serious undertaking. Every now and then the *sofer* would receive some money on account to send home to his family and cover expenses.

The *Sefer Torah* was finally completed. The scribe went

in to Reb Shimon to tell him the good news and to ask for the balance of his fee. Reb Shimon was overjoyed.

"How much have I already paid you on account?" he asked.

The scribe took out a small notebook and began reading: "In April I received this amount... In May so much and so much... In June..."

The Baron cut him short. "Really!" he thundered at him. "Is that how a *sofer* reckons the months? According to their Christian names?! Could you not have recorded the same information according to the Jewish months or at least according to the weekly *parashiyos*? You, a person who labors in holy work all day long, who has no need for Christian notations, a so-called learned man, don't you know that the Torah forbids even mention of these gentile and heathen names?!"

Red with rage, the Baron counted out the remainder of the sum he owed and paid it to the Russian scribe. Then, in anger he said, "Go! And when you leave, take your *Sefer Torah* along with you! I don't want it!"

Surprise in His Hand

וְהָיָה לְךָ לְאוֹת עַל יָדְךָ וּלְזִכָּרוֹן בֵּין עֵינֶיךָ

And it shall be to you for a sign on your arm and a memorial between your eyes (13:9)

The Romans made life very difficult for the Jews in *Eretz Yisrael.* They passed all kinds of laws to make them forget their religion; to make them more like the

Romans. But the Jews disobeyed these laws and flaunted Roman rule. One of these harsh laws was the ban on putting on *tefillin*. Whoever would do so was to be put to death.

Elisha Hatzaddik, who lived at this time, was such a holy person that he wore his *tefillin* all day long, inside his house and even when he went out.

When the evil decree was passed, he continued putting on his *tefillin* daily. He loved this commandment so much that he was willing to risk his life for it. Elisha would put on his *tefillin* early in the morning, in the *beis knesses*, and then go around with them all day, even in the central marketplace.

One morning, as he was coming back from the *beis knesses*, he suddenly caught the attention of a Roman soldier passing by, patrolling the streets. Elisha saw the soldier and began running towards his home where he hoped to hide his *tefillin* before he was caught.

As soon as the soldier saw Elisha pick up his heels, he pursued him. The soldier soon overtook the Sage. When Elisha heard the soldier's footsteps behind him, he said a quick prayer, "Please, *Hashem*, perform a miracle to save me!" While on the run, he wrenched the *tefillin* off his head and arm, and grasped them tightly in his hand.

A minute later the soldier gripped him from behind and forced him to stop. "Halt, Jew! I just saw you walking along with *tefillin* on your head. Where did you hide them? What are you holding in your hand?"

"Pigeon wings," said Elisha, holding his fist tightly shut.

"I don't believe you!" the Roman shouted. "Open up your hand and show me what you are hiding there!"

Elisha held out his hand. There in his palm nestled a pair of white pigeon wings! A miracle had occurred and the *tefillin* had been changed into pigeon wings!

The soldier could hardly believe his eyes. But there was no doubt about it. There were the soft white bird wings, not black *tefillin*.

From that time on Elisha was called: Elisha of the Pigeon Wings.

(According to Tractate *Shabbos 49a*)

The Inheritance

וְהָיָה לְךָ לְאוֹת עַל יָדְךָ וּלְזִכָּרוֹן בֵּין עֵינֶיךָ

And it shall be to you for a sign on your arm and a memorial between your eyes (13:9)

R' Yisrael of Ruzhin was mourned by everyone when he departed this world but most of all by his four sons. When it came to dividing up the inheritance, the brothers were at a loss. In the end it was agreed to apportion the Rebbe's effects by lottery. R' David Moshe of Chortkov was awarded the priceless *tefillin* his father had inherited from their grandfather, the Maggid of Mezeritch. He was overjoyed.

When everything was duly divided up, the oldest brother, R' Avraham Yaakov of Sadigura, said, "Now that everything is taken care of, I am curious to know what each of us desired most."

R′ David Moshe said that he would have laid aside all claim to anything as long as he received R′ Yisrael′s *tefillin*. The other brothers saw that *Hashem* had fulfilled the will of the righteous.

R′ Meir Shapira of Lublin had another story to tell about these *tefillin*:

About two years after his father′s passing, the Sadigura Rebbe sat amongst his chasidim. They had just lit *Chanukah* candles when suddenly the Rebbe commented, "How I envy my brother the *tefillin* with which he prays, the pair that once belonged to our grandfather, the holy Maggid of Mezeritch!"

Suddenly, the gathering noticed that two young men turned pale. One of them said, "Rebbe, we must confess to something terrible. We both knew how the Rebbe yearned for those *tefillin*. We secretly removed the *parashiyos* and replaced them with inferior *parashiyos*. We have waited to confess this to the Rebbe for a long time. We felt that we had not done the right thing and were afraid to give them to you."

Then they went home to fetch the holy *parashiyos*.

Everyone looked at one another, stunned. How had they dared to commit such a sneaky, dishonorable act? And how had R′ David Moshe not sensed anything amiss?

They all sat in silence until the young men returned. The Rebbe took the *parashiyos* from them and made everyone present promise not to breathe a word of what they had just learned.

Right after *Chanukah* the Rebbe went to Potik to visit

his brother, accompanied by that same group of chasidim.

On the morning after their arrival R' Avraham Yaakov went into his brother's room and saw two pairs of *tefillin* lying on the table, one of them, the pair that he had inherited from his father. The Sadigura Rebbe watched as his brother went over to the table and took his father's *tefillin*. He sighed deeply and bitterly, then set them aside, turning to the second pair, which he put on.

When R' Avraham Yaakov saw this, he turned to his brother and asked, "Why don't you put on 'the *Tatte*'s *tefillin*?"

"I'll tell you the truth, dear brother," he confided with a sigh. "Throughout the two years that they have been in my possession, I have not worn them once. Each time that I take them in my hand I feel, somehow, that I am not worthy of them, and so, I put them back without donning them. I recite the blessing and pray with a different pair."

"Oh no, dear brother!" the Sadigura Rebbe hastened to comfort him. "You are wrong in thinking that you are unworthy. That is not the reason at all! If you do not feel any special sanctity in that pair it is because the *parashiyos* have been removed. Here they are. Put them back where they belong."

During the First World War when the Cossacks burned down the *beis medrash* of the Chortkover Rebbe and plundered all that they could lay their hands on, the precious *tefillin* were lost. Eventually, though, they were miraculously retrieved, and thanks to special distinguishing marks, were returned to their holy owner.

Letters Flying in the Air

וְהָיָה לְךָ לְאוֹת עַל יָדְךָ וּלְזִכָּרוֹן בֵּין עֵינֶיךָ לְמַעַן תִּהְיֶה תּוֹרַת ה׳ בְּפִיךָ

And they shall be to you for a sign on your arm and a memorial between your eyes so that the Torah of Hashem shall be in your mouth (13:9)

R' Chaim ben Attar, the Or Hachayim, lay on his deathbed. The best doctors had been called in to treat him, but to no avail. In a short while he would leave the world.

His wife approached the bed. With tear-swollen eyes, she cried, "Dear husband! When you leave me, I will be all alone in the world. Who will sustain me? What will become of me?"

R' Chaim gathered his last ounce of strength and whispered to her, "Do not fear, my good woman, my loyal wife and helpmate. I will not allow you to starve. After I die a rich man will come here from Constantinople. He will offer you three hundred *ducats* for my *tefillin*. Accept that sum, for it will be enough to last you for the rest of your life. You will be able to live in comfort. But, you must remember one vital thing:" Here he paused for a rest, then continued, "Tell him, in my name, that when he wears my *tefillin*, he must never divert his thoughts from them. He must never utter any phrase or word that does not directly apply to prayer. Warn him about this; don't forget!"

R' Chaim lay back in his bed, his strength spent. His

wife was comforted. In a few moments, his holy soul parted from its earthly body.

All of Jerusalem mourned the passing of the great man. When the mourning period was over a rich man came to the widow offering to buy the Or Hachayim's *tefillin* for three hundred *ducats*. Remembering her husband's words, she agreed. But before she handed them over to him, she repeated her husband's last warning, "Make sure to concentrate all of your thoughts only on prayer while you are wearing these *tefillin*. Do not talk or think of anything other than the prayers."

The man thanked her and took his precious package back home to Turkey. He was extremely careful to purify his thoughts when he was wearing the valuable *tefillin*. How fervently he prayed! How precious the *tefillin* were to him! How lovingly he placed them on his head and wound the straps around his arm!

One time, however, as he was sitting in the *beis knesses*, one of his young servants came to tell him of an important customer who was waiting for him at the shop. At first, he was too engrossed to even notice the servant, but when the boy persisted, he uttered a sharp word before returning to his prayers.

From then on things were not the same. The rich man felt a change in his prayers. All the sanctity he had felt up until then while wearing the *tefillin* was gone! He was deeply disturbed as soon as he realized this, but could not pinpoint the cause. He certainly did not attribute the change to that one sharp word he had spoken. He innocently thought that perhaps some letter in the *tefillin* had been erased and decided to take the *tefillin* to a master *sofer* to be checked.

As soon as the *sofer* opened up the *tefillin* and removed

the *parashiyos,* he gaped in shock. He placed the parchment before the owner's eyes and he, too, stared openmouthed, aghast at the terrible sight. The parchment was smooth, as if nothing had ever been written on it at all! Not one letter was visible! They had all disappeared, vanished into thin air.

The Squarer Rebbe told this story to his own chasidim and, when he reached the conclusion, rose and said emotionally, "At the very moment that the rich man took his attention away from the *tefillin* and turned to daily matters, at that moment the holy letters left the parchment, one by one, and flew up into the air, straight back to heaven."

Take the Other Road

הִרְבָּה כּוֹשֵׁל גַּם נָפַל אִישׁ אֶל רֵעֵהוּ וַיֹּאמְרוּ קוּמָה וְנָשֻׁבָה

He made many to stumble, yes, they fell one upon another and said: Arise and let us return

(Haftorah Parashas Bo, Yirmiyahu 46)

It was *Yom Kippur* eve, the night of *Kol Nidre.* As usual, the Yismach Moshe addressed his congregation, exhorting them to abandon their false and wicked practices and repent wholeheartedly. In conclusion, he said, "You may ask why I don't repent as well, why I am not the perfect example. To this question I will reply with a short story: A man once lost his way in the forest.

When he met up with another man, he rushed up to him eagerly and asked, 'How does one get out of this place?' To which the other replied, 'I am afraid that I cannot tell you that. I am also lost and do not know the way out myself. But one thing I can tell you — don't take the path that I just took.' "

The Parable of the Chickens

אֶעֱשֶׂה כָלָה בְּכָל הַגּוֹיִם אֲשֶׁר הִדַּחְתִּיךָ שָׁמָּה, וְאֹתְךָ
לֹא אֶעֱשֶׂה כָלָה

For I will completely destroy all the nations where I have driven you, but I will not destroy you completely
(Haftorah Parashas Bo, Yirmiyah 46)

A king once challenged a Jewish rabbi: "I am surprised at you Jews," he said. "You are so intelligent and yet so stubborn. You believe in one G-d and in the coming of a Messiah. But just look at the world, look at human nature and try to picture what would happen if one single person came along and tried to impose his rule over all the nations of the world. Who could possibly please everyone, or be strong enough to subjugate everyone? It is illogical and unnatural. Nations are different and people everywhere are different. It would simply be an impossible feat."

"Give me a few days," the rabbi asked, "and I will give

you an answer."

The king agreed. He was curious to see how the rabbi would convince him that one man could rule the entire world. The allotted time passed and the rabbi appeared before the king. He said, "In order to prove my point, I need seventy plump and sturdy roosters and a little scrawny one. Can you supply these for me by tomorrow?"

The king's curiosity was aroused and he agreed. Early the next morning, the rabbi came and placed all the birds together in one large hall and ordered that they be starved for the entire day and night.

The following morning the rabbi and the king came to see how the roosters were faring. The rabbi opened a window of the hall and threw in a handful of chicken feed.

Pandemonium reigned. The hungry birds pounced on the small handful of seeds. But, since there was not enough to go around, they began fighting among themselves. The roosters screeched at the top of their lungs; feathers flew; blood spurted. The food was forgotten.

As soon as the fight began, the scrawny rooster ran for cover under a chair in the corner of the room. There, no one paid any attention to him. The rest of the roosters fought to the finish, scratching and screeching, clawing and crowing. It was all over very soon. Dead and wounded chickens were strewn all over the floor. There was not one survivor who had the strength to even claim the spoils of war. They all lay there, bleeding, wings broken and crops torn off.

After a few minutes, the only healthy bird began to poke his head out from under the chair and see if all was clear. No one challenged him now, as he walked out and began pecking among the untouched grain. More and more confidently, he strode among the battle victims like a king, claiming all the food for himself.

The king and the rabbi watched the strange scene silently. The rabbi then spoke up, "Do you see that, Your Majesty? That scrawny, weak rooster can be compared to the *Mashiach*. In future times *Hashem* will cause all the seventy nations of the world to challenge one another in a world war. They will throw themselves into the fray, much as you saw these brawny roosters fighting. No one will be the victor; they will all emerge mortally wounded. *Mashiach* will then appear on the scene to claim the spoils of war and no one will have the strength or interest to challenge or stop him. He, alone, will rule over all the nations and will redeem us from their hands.

פָּרָשַׁת בְּשַׁלַּח

Parashas Beshalach

Right in the Torah

אֲשֶׁר רְאִיתֶם אֶת מִצְרַיִם הַיּוֹם לֹא תֹסִפוּ לִרְאוֹתָם עוֹד

As you have seen Egypt today, you shall never see them again (14:13)

All of the great rabbis of Poland had been approached and been asked the unusual question.

Two brothers had once been partners in a business, but had broken off on bad terms. One of them had sworn that he did not want to see the other ever again. But, when his brother died, he regretted his rash vow and wished to beg forgiveness at the graveside. Was the vow still binding after the brother's death or was it not? That was the question.

The rabbis thrashed the problem out. Proofs were brought from the Talmud and from *poskim*, pro and con. But they could not agree upon a decision.

This interesting question reached the ears of twelve-year-old Yechezkel Landau, who would later grow up to be the famous rabbi of Prague and world-renowned *halachic* authority known for his work, *Noda BeYehuda*. The child was gifted with an astute mind and saw a clear solution at once. He said, "I am surprised that the rabbis have not found the answer to this problem right in the Torah!"

"What do you mean?" he was asked.

"It is stated clearly in *Parashas Beshalach*. Moshe Rabbenu told the Jews that they would never see the Egyptians again as they saw them then. And yet only a few verses later we find that 'Israel saw Egypt dead on the shores of the sea.' It is apparent that seeing someone dead is not the same as seeing him alive. Thus, the vow which the man made never to see his brother again does not apply now that his brother is dead."

The Ginai River

וַיִּבָּקְעוּ הַמָּיִם

And the waters parted (14:21)

R' Pinchas ben Yair was especially devoted to the commandment of *pidyon shevuyim,* ransoming Jewish prisoners. He put much time into collecting funds to buy off Jewish slaves from gentile captors.

On one of his trips, he met a Jew traveling in the same direction. The latter was bringing sacks of wheat to be ground into flour for *matzos* for *Pesach*. Both agreed that it was safer and more pleasant to ride in company and so, they traveled together.

Along the way the two Jews met up with an Arab

merchant who was carrying goods for sale. He greeted them and asked if he could join their party. They agreed. The three traveled together until they reached the Ginai River.

Normally, the river was a slow-moving one, shallow and easily crossed even on a donkey's back. But now it was swollen with winter rains. It was overflowing its banks and its turbulent waters swept everything along in their path. The travelers realized at once that they could not cross it by swimming or on the back of a donkey — and there was no bridge.

R' Pinchas was in a hurry. He was afraid that if he did not get to the captives on time they would be sold or taken far away. Their lives were in danger! He stood on the banks of the rushing river and cried out, "Ginai! Ginai! Divide so that I may cross over. I am going to perform a *mitzvah,* to redeem Jewish captives!"

From the rushing, gushing waters a gurgling voice could suddenly be heard: 'You wish to carry out the will of the Creator. I, too, execute the will of the Creator by flowing. In the beginning of Creation I was commanded to flow on and on; this is what I have been dutifully doing since then. You might not succeed in carrying out your task. Many different things can come up to prevent you from freeing those captives while I, every minute that I flow, am fulfilling my destiny. No! I cannot divide my waters for you."

Undaunted, R' Pinchas threatened, "If you do not divide your waters for me, I will decree that you stop flowing forever more!"

At that moment, the river divided. The waters running downstream continued on their tumultuous way while the water that reached R' Pinchas halted and rose up in a wall, while he crossed over safely to the other side.

Before he had reached it, though, he heard a voice behind him, "Rebbe," said the man with the wheat, "What shall I do? I cannot cross the river for I am afraid that my wheat will get wet and will be unfit for baking *matzah*. It will become *chametz!*"

R' Pinchas turned back to the river and said, "Allow this Jew to cross, too, for he is, also, going to perform a *mitzvah*." The river remained still, while the Jew crossed over.

Their traveling companion, the Arab merchant, still remained behind. R' Pinchas caught sight of him and cried out, "Ginai, let the Arab merchant cross as well for he is our traveling companion. Let him cross, too, lest he say that we abandoned him." And so the Arab merchant crossed over, thanks to R' Pinchas ben Yair.

Only when the three were safely on the other side did the high wall of water tumble down and the Ginai River resume its course.

(According to Tractate *Chulin* 7a)

Two Notes

וַיַּאֲמִינוּ בַּה׳ וּבְמֹשֶׁה עַבְדּוֹ

And they believed in Hashem and in Moshe His servant (14:31)

Berel and Baruch were good friends who lived in neighboring villages. While Berel put great stock in chasidic Rebbes and their blessings, his friend, Baruch, did not believe in them at all. Not so their wives. Berel's wife had no faith in Rebbes while Baruch's had implicit faith

in every word they spoke.

It happened that Berel fell ill. He consulted many doctors, but none were able to help him and he appealed to his family to go to the Rebbe for a blessing. Although Berel's wife was reluctant to do so, she did want her husband to get well and she wished to do everything in her power to please him. And so, she agreed to go to Ruzhin to ask R' Yisrael for his blessing.

She set out on the journey which took her through the village where Baruch lived. Poor Baruch did not have a penny to his name and his yearly rent for his inn was soon due. When Baruch's wife learned that her friend was going to the Ruzhiner Rebbe, she decided to go along and ask him for his blessing. She believed with all her heart that the *tzaddik* would be able to help her.

When the two women arrived they were led into a waiting room. There they prepared their *kvitlach*, notes, for the Rebbe, describing their troubles. By some strange quirk of fate, the two notes got mixed up.

Berel's wife handed the Rebbe a note begging him to pray for funds. R' Yisrael scanned the note and said, "May *Hashem* send you His salvation." Berel's wife left and went home to reassure her husband that the Rebbe had blessed him.

Baruch's wife submitted the note to the Rebbe asking for a speedy recovery. He read that and advised, "Apply leeches and everything will turn out alright."

While this should have sounded like strange advice for a man who was not ill, Baruch's wife, who believed in the Rebbe's divine intuition, asked no questions. When she reached home, she told her husband what the Rebbe had said. Baruch, the skeptic, shrugged his shoulders and said, "While I am doubtful that it can help, it surely can do no harm to try."

When the day for his payment arrived, Baruch went to bed and applied leeches. Poor Baruch lay in bed, moaning with pain, his body bruised and bloody.

Just then someone pounded on the door. It was an officer of the law sent to collect Baruch's payment. He asked to be shown to the master of the house. Baruch's wife led him to the bedroom. The policeman saw Baruch writhing in pain. After stating his message, he went back to the landlord to report what he had seen.

"I don't believe it," the landlord said. "Just yesterday I saw him roaming the streets, hale and hearty. He could not have taken ill so suddenly. He must be pretending in order to get out of his payment. Bring him here at once, ill or not."

The policeman got someone to help him and together they transported Baruch — bed and all — to the landlord's house. As they carried the bed into the courtyard, the landlord's wife happened to look out of the window and saw Baruch, whom she knew well, writhing in pain. She rushed out to see what this was all about. Her husband also appeared on the scene, demanding to know what had happened.

Suddenly Baruch had an idea and said, "I went to the city yesterday to try to borrow money to pay my rent, which I knew was due today. I went to relatives and friends and after much effort succeeded in assembling the entire sum. It was my bad luck that the last coach to the village had just left. I had no choice but to go by foot. When I was some way out of the city I was suddenly attacked from behind. Robbers burst out of the forest and pounced upon me. They beat me mercilessly until I fell to the ground. They went through my pockets and took all my money.

I don't know how I made it home. I stumbled and staggered until I collapsed at my front door. I was carried into the house and have lain in bed, unable to leave it, or even move my limbs. I don't know what I will do now. Not only do I owe the rent, but I have all those debts to pay back to my friends and relatives who lent me the money."

Berel buried his head in his hands and wept, but only partly, in pretence. He really did not know what he was going to do.

The landlord's wife was overcome with sympathy. "You poor fellow!" Turning to her husband accusingly, she said, "It is all your fault, you know. All this happened to Baruch because he wanted to pay his rent. We must do something for him."

Turning back to the bedridden Baruch, she said, "Don't worry. Your debt for the rent is cancelled, that's for sure. As for the money you borrowed, we will take care of that too. And in addition, we will let you have the inn rent-free for the next three years."

The landlord nodded in agreement. Thus Baruch, who had followed the Rebbe's advice reluctantly, was repaid twice and three times over.

As for Berel, he soon recovered his good health.

R' Aharon of Karlin told this story in the name of the Ruzhiner Rebbe who had blessed the two women. In conclusion, he would say:

"This is what R' Yisrael told me: 'Believe me, when I read the note about the rent money I had not the faintest idea how to help the woman. But she, in her devout and fervent faith, her *emunas chachamim*, forced Heaven to help her. She herself brought about her salvation.' "

The Specialist From Anipoli

כִּי אֲנִי ה׳ רֹפְאֶךָ

For I am Hashem, Your physician (15:26)

"Please, Rebbe, you must help me," wept the stricken Jew before R' Mordechai of Neschiz.

"What is your trouble?" the kind and patient Rebbe asked sympathetically.

"I am mortally ill. My doctors say that I do not have long to live. I have consulted the best physicians but none of them hold out any hope for me. My illness, they say, is incurable. Only you can help me, Rebbe, now that all hope is gone!"

"Hmmm. And have you been to the specialist from Anipoli yet?" asked the Rebbe.

The ill man wrinkled his forehead in surprise. "Strange, but I never heard of him before. No, I have not been to see him."

"Well then, you should go to him at once."

With hope rekindled in his heart, the dying man packed a few belongings and went to Anipoli. The journey was long and arduous, not at all comfortable even for a well person. The coach jostled him back and forth; the night lodgings were dirty and the food they offered skimpy. But the man did not mind. He kept on thinking that his salvation was only two days journey away, then one day away. Finally he reached the small village of Anipoli.

He jumped out of the coach; he already felt better. He grabbed the the sleeve of the first passerby and asked, "Can you tell me where the specialist lives?" The man looked at him in bewilderment. "Specialist? Here, in Anipoli? There is no specialist living here! You must be mistaken."

"There is no mistake. A great man sent me here to consult the specialist about my illness. You are the one who is uninformed."

He turned away from the passerby and found another local resident. "Perhaps you can tell me where the specialist of Anipoli lives?" he asked. This man looked at him as if he were crazy.

"Are you mad? A specialist in this little backwater town? Why we don't even have our own doctor. Which doctor would want to settle here?"

He could not understand it. "But I was told that a famous specialist lived here..." he muttered in despair. By now, he realized that he was the one who had made the mistake. Still, the Rebbe had told him to come here. There must be some explanation.

"Well, then, what do you do here when someone becomes ill?" he asked falteringly.

"Now that is a different question altogether," the man said. "If someone falls ill, we pray to *Hashem* to cure him. It is as simple as that!"

Crestfallen, the Jew saw that he had nothing to seek here any longer and took the first coach back to Neschiz.

He returned to R' Mordechai and poured out his painful story to him. "There is no specialist in Anipoli," he wept. "There is not even a general practitioner there. My trip was all in vain!"

The Rebbe raised his eyebrows questioningly. "And

what do people do when someone becomes ill? Did you find out?"

"Yes," the unhappy Jew replied weakly. "Since they have no doctor, they pray to *Hashem* to cure them."

"Aha!" said the Rebbe triumphantly. "That is the answer. That is the specialist that I wanted you to consult. *Hashem*! He is the ultimate Healer. He is the one to Whom you must turn in your suffering and pain for only He can help you! As it says in the Torah — 'For I am *Hashem* Your Healer'."

The Mitzvah on Trial

אֲנַסֶּנּוּ הֲיֵלֵךְ בְּתוֹרָתִי

I shall test him whether he will follow My teachings (16:4)

Reb Zundel was a successful innkeeper. He was conscientious and earned the respect of his customers and the trust of his landlord. He had everything he could want except that which money cannot buy — children. He and his wife were childless.

Once, his landlord summoned him and presented him with an offer. "I am about to move away to a different district and wish to liquidate my property. Since I regard you so highly, I would like to give you the first opportunity of buying the inn which you rent from me as well as all the land on which it stands, a considerable estate, for only one tenth of its value. I want the payment made in cash since I will be traveling. If you can produce the sum in a week, the inn and its property is all yours. It is a bargain which I surely advise you not to overlook!"

The Jew heard his offer and was elated. What a golden opportunity! To own the inn! He had never dreamed of such wealth! How could he pass up such a chance? And yet, the sum which the landlord requested, even though it was a fraction of the estate's worth, was a considerable one. It was more cash than he could gather.

Reb Zundel left the landlord's mansion and walked home slowly. He was sunk deep in thought. His wife might have a suggestion. And she did. "We own our own home, don't forget. Let's sell it! If I sell all of our silver and my jewelry and perhaps borrow some money from friends, I am sure that we can come up with that sum. It is a sure investment. We cannot go wrong! It is a once-in-a-lifetime chance!"

Reb Zundel agreed. Quickly they raised the cash and Reb Zundel went off to the landlord to make the purchase.

He set out with a light foot and a happy heart. But as he walked along, his ears caught the sound of weeping. It was coming from a cottage by the side of the road.

Reb Zundel turned towards the cottage and walked in.

What a sight met his eyes! On the floor lay the body of a dead man, surrounded by his widow, and seven children. They were weeping bitterly. Their father had died and left them destitue.

Tears gathered in Reb Zundel's eyes. With one dramatic gesture, he thrust the sack of money at the widow and urged, "Take it! It will support you and your children for a long time to come!"

The widow looked at the money, not believing her eyes. Where had this man come from? Was he teasing her with that huge sum of money? At first she refused to touch it, but, when he assured her that he meant it with all his heart, she finally agreed.

This generous deed made a deep impression in Heaven. A Jew had sacrificed his future to help strangers, a widow and her orphans. What a magnanimous deed! What a tremendous sacrifice! He had given her a veritable fortune, a gesture which left him penniless! The heavenly court ruled that this man must be rewarded on earth with some wonderful gift.

When Satan heard about the decision, he objected. "Before a man is rewarded with a great gift from the heavenly treasury, he must first be tested to see if his goodness is genuine. I will test him myself. If he withstands the trial, he may be rewarded with the prize."

The heavenly court could not deny that Satan had a valid point. But Eliyahu Hanavi came to Reb Zundel's defense. "If he must be tested, I want to administer the test, for Satan may put him to a very difficult trial which he will not withstand. That would not be fair. I will arrange an impartial trial."

This suggestion pleased the heavenly court and Eliyahu was allowed to descend to earth to test Reb Zundel.

After Reb Zundel had given all of his money to the widow, he did not have the heart to go home. He decided to go far away, to a different city, where he was not known. Perhaps, he would find his fortune this way.

Reb Zundel walked and walked, until by evening he had reached the edge of a city. Since he did not know anyone there, he went directly to the *beis medrash*. He was determined not to ask for charity, but wait until someone offered him something to eat and a place to sleep. Hungry and tired, he sat down by a table in the *beis medrash* and opened up a *sefer.* He was soon deeply engrossed in it and did not even notice that an old man, venerable and distinguished-looking, had entered and approached him. He spoke to Reb Zundel kindly, "*Shalom aleichem*! And where do you come from? What are you doing here, in our city?"

Warmed by his kind tone, Reb Zundel told about himself. In the course of the conversation he mentioned the deed he had done just that morning. The old man listened openmouthed.

"Amazing!" he murmured. "I have an offer to make you."

Reb Zundel wondered, "What kind of offer?"

The old man continued, "You see, I am an old man and very well off. What would you say if I offered you a large sum of money, enough to support you and your wife comfortably till the end of your days? All I want in exchange is the reward for the *mitzvah* that you did when you helped the widow." When he saw that Reb Zundel was not at all interested, he added, "Look at it this way; if you are well-to-do, you will be able to help many widows and orphans for the rest of your life. Surely you cannot turn this offer down!"

At first, it seemed to Reb Zundel, as if he were dreaming. *Hashem* had answered his prayers so quickly? He was almost about to open his mouth and accept when a different thought went through his mind. "How can I do such a thing? If *Hashem* was good enough to let this deed come my way, how can I give it up so quickly? It is not every day that one has a chance to make such a selfless sacrifice on such a large scale." And he replied to the old man, "No, I cannot accept your kind offer. Not for all the money in the world!"

"If you are unwilling to part with the entire *mitzvah,*" said the old man, changing his proposition somewhat, "then sell me part of it, at least. I will pay handsomely for even a small portion, up to half of my fortune!"

Reb Zundel stood firm. He would not sell even half of his good deed. The old man did not give up. "Please," he begged. "Sell me just one tiny part, say one percent, no more. Just as long as I have a share in that worthy gesture. Please!"

"No! No! That is final! Not even the tiniest speck of it. I want the credit all for myself; it was my sacrifice. I don't want to hear another word about it."

The old man rose and with a benign smile on his face said, "Listen to me: I am Eliyahu Hanavi. I have been sent to you from Heaven to put you to a test. Not only were you worthy of doing that good deed to begin with but you withstood the test absolutely. As a reward, Heaven is willing to grant you one of three things: long life for you and your wife, success and great wealth, or a son who will someday light up the world with his Torah and piety."

Without even hesitating, Reb Zundel replied, "I want a son. As you must know, my wife and I are childless. Of what use is long life or riches, if we have no children?"

Eliyahu Hanavi nodded happily. It was a wise decision. "Very well. Next year, by this time, you will be blessed with a son. But this promise has one condition attached to it."

"What is that?"

'You and your wife must live a nomad's life, constantly wandering, on the go, in exile for the rest of your lives."

"I must first ask my wife before giving you my decision," Reb Zundel said. He returned home and received her wholehearted approval.

Reb Zundel and his wife embarked upon their lives as wandering paupers. Within a year they were blessed with a son whom they called Menachem. This Menachem grew up to be the famous Menachem Mendel of Riminov who graced the world with his Torah and righteousness.

The Honor and the Glory

וְנַחְנוּ מָה
What do we amount to? (16:7)

What grand preparations! All of Warsaw was festively bedecked for the rabbinical convention that was to take place. What an honor it was for the community to host such great figures as R' Akiva Eiger and R' Yaakov Lauberbaum of Lisa, men renowned for their scholarship and *midos.*

The day arrived. Soon the coach bearing these two *tzaddikim* would make its way through the festooned streets of Warsaw to the cheers of the crowd. People were beside themselves with excitement and joy.

The coach could be seen in the distance. The crowd surged forward. Suddenly, someone unhitched the horses, grabbed hold of one of the shafts and began pulling the coach. Others quickly followed suit and soon the wagon was being pulled forward by the people themselves.

Inside sat R' Akiva Eiger in one corner and R' Yaakov

in the other, both deeply immersed in their thoughts. R' Akiva Eiger was a modest, humble person and did not even dream that all this honor might be for him. Was not R' Yaakov in this coach? This exuberant welcome must be for him. Oh how R' Akiva longed to join them and show his deep regard for R' Yaakov. He slipped quietly out of the door on his side and began pulling the wagon along. Now he felt happy! Now he was giving honor to the Torah and its scholars.

R' Yaakov was having similar thoughts. He, too, did not dream that the grand welcome was for him. R' Akiva was by far the greater man. He, too, wished to show his respect for this Torah leader. And so R' Yaakov also slipped out of the coach and joined the crowd.

In the great crush, no one noticed these two small figures. Singing and hailing the historic event, the people pulled the heavy coach through the city streets, unaware that they were honoring an empty carriage. No one realized the error until they reached the hotel where the two would be lodging. Then they saw the empty vehicle and realized what had happened.

Joy — Reserved for Shabbos

אִכְלֻהוּ הַיּוֹם כִּי שַׁבָּת הַיּוֹם

Eat it today for today is Shabbos (16:25)

R' Nosson David of Shidlowitz was once staying at a health resort when he ran out of funds. The *shammash* who attended to all of the Rebbe's needs was deeply concerned, but he was certain that by *Shabbos* some of the Rebbe's richer chasidim would come to join them, to be with the Rebbe for the holy day. They would come to his aid.

The *shammash* was not to be disappointed, for on Thursday a rich chasid did come to the spa to spend the *Shabbos* with the Rebbe. The *shammash* rushed to tell him of the Rebbe's predicament and, as he had expected, the chasid gladly gave him a large sum.

The *shammash* thanked him profusely and ran to tell the Rebbe the good news.

Later that day the chasid was shown in to see the Rebbe. To his amazement, the Rebbe hardly looked at him. He said a weak "*Shalom aleichem*" and turned away to other business. The chasid was deeply disappointed and hurt. Was this the welcome that he deserved after he had given the Rebbe such a large sum? But, far worse than the pain was the thought that the Rebbe was ungrateful.

Thursday passed. Friday came. Then it was Friday night. After the prayers, R' Nosson David beckoned to the rich chasid. "*Shalom aleichem, Gut Shabbos*!" he said, with warmth and joy. "How happy I am to see you. How glad I am that you came for *Shabbos!*" In reply to the astonished look on the chasid's face, he explained, "You must be surprised that I saved my warm greeting only for now. You are surely wondering why I did not greet you enthusiastically when you arrived, especially since you gave such a generous donation when I was so pressed for money. Let me explain. I wished to experience this joy on *Shabbos*, the holy day of rest and joy. I took that joy and set it aside so that I could experience it today. And now you see how truly happy I am to have you here with me!"

Why Is One Day Different?

אַל יֵצֵא אִישׁ מִמְּקֹמוֹ בַּיּוֹם הַשְּׁבִיעִי

Let no man leave his place on the seventh day (16:29)

Turnus Rufus, the Roman, loved to bait the Jews and challenge them with his questions. One time he met R' Akiva on the street. It was *Shabbos.*

"Why is one day different from another?" he asked him.

R' Akiva was not puzzled. He replied with a question of his own, "Why is one man different from another?"

Turnus Rufus was confused. He did not know what R' Akiva had in mind and he asked, "What is the connection between my question and yours?"

R' Akiva explained, You asked why the *Shabbos* was singled out from all other days of the week. I asked in return why you are different from ordinary people."

Turnus Rufus thrust his chest out and boasted, "What a question! Of course I am different. I rule over thousands of men. I deserve to be honored!"

"The same applies to the *Shabbos*!" R' Akiva said. "It is singled out from other days because the King of kings, the A-mighty Creator, set it aside as a special day. He willed it thus!"

Turnus Rufus was determined to have the last word. "If that is so, why does He work on *Shabbos*?"

"What work does He do?" R' Akiva asked. Turnus Rufus replied, "He does exactly what He does during the week; He makes the wind blow, the rain fall, the clouds travel, the sun shine. He causes fruits and vegetables to grow. Everything, everything just as it is on a weekday!"

R' Akiva replied, "I know that Your Excellency is expert in many Jewish laws and customs. Let me use an analogy from Jewish law. Let us say that there are two Jews who live together in one narrow courtyard. Their courtyard is not united by an *eruv*, however, and they are forbidden to carry from one house to the other even though the distance is short. In contrast, another Jew, a rich man, who owns a large palace with a huge courtyard, as large as an entire county is permitted to carry things from one end of his courtyard to another, for it is his private property. The same applies to *Hashem*. The heavens are His throne and the earth is His footstool. The entire world is filled with His glory. It is His private domain, His private property. Surely He is allowed to carry and move things about within his own boundaries!"

(Midrash Tanchuma Ki Sisa 33)

Rebuke — For Some

מַה תְּרִיבוּן עִמָּדִי מַה תְּנַסּוּן אֶת ה׳

Why do you quarrel with me; why do you test Hashem (17:2)

R' Yisrael Salanter was forced to travel around considerably. Whenever he traveled along a certain road, he made sure to stop over at the inn of a certain G-d fearing Jew for a meal and a rest.

Upon one of his visits he noticed, to his horror, that the innkeeper had some salami of doubtful *kashrus* upon his table!

Always one to find good in a person, he thought that someone must have deceived him into thinking that the salami was permissible. He decided to speak to him.

When R' Yisrael told him that the salami was possibly not kosher, the innkeeper replied, "Oh, I know. But of late, I have not been so careful about my *mitzvah*-observance. I now eat things of doubtful *kashrus*."

Now R' Yisrael was shocked. "What has made you change so suddenly? You were such a decent, G-d fearing Jew! How did such a terrible thing happen?"

The naive innkeeper told R' Yisrael about the visitor who had come to his inn and convinced him, by various 'proofs' that there was no Creator, G-d forbid, no Providence in this world.

"What kind of proofs did he give you?" asked R' Yisrael.

"He took a slice of this salami, held it up and said to me, 'If I eat this unkosher meat and am struck dead, that would prove that there is a G-d Who sees and punishes. But if I eat it and nothing happens to me, it is proof that there is no G-d on earth and that one may do as one pleases!'

"He then took a bite. I waited but nothing at all happened. He stood there, just as before, unharmed. Since then, I, too, have been eating non-kosher meat. Why not?"

R' Yisrael had listened to the story in bitter silence. What could he say? He found it difficult to talk to the ignorant innkeeper.

A short while later, the innkeeper's young daughter burst into the room, waving an official-looking certificate. "Look, Father!" she cried proudly. "I just got a certificate of excellence for my musical talent. Isn't that wonderful?"

Her father praised her highly and held the certificate up high for all to see.

When the excitement had calmed down, R' Yisrael called the young girl over to his table and said, "I noticed that you just received a certificate of honor for your excellent playing. I don't believe that you are such a fine musician at all. Prove it to me."

The girl refused to play before this stranger and left the room in a huff. R' Yisrael got up and went over to her father, the innkeeper, complaining, "Your daughter lacks basic courtesy! I just asked her to play for me but she refused."

"I will call her at once," said the embarrassed father.

When his daughter stood before them, he asked, "Why did you refuse to play before this guest?"

She replied petulantly, "I have already amply proven my musical talent and ability in school. That is how I received the certificate. But, that does not mean that I must prove myself over and over again before any and every curious person who asks me to play for him!"

"Aha!" R' Yisrael exulted. "There is your answer! Your little girl is far wiser than you! *Hashem* redeemed us from Egyptian slavery, performed marvelous miracles for us, split the sea and drowned our enemies. He gave us the *manna* in the desert and so on. Are all these miracles not enough proof of His ability, proof that He created and guides the world? Certainly these acts are proof enough for all generations of *Hashem*'s divine Providence! Why must He prove Himself over and over again for every peasant and wastrel, like that salami eater?!"

The innkeeper bowed his head in shame. He realized his gross mistake and got rid of the *treife* meat immediately.

The Deceit of the Rich

בִּפְרֹעַ פְּרָעוֹת בְּיִשְׂרָאֵל בְּהִתְנַדֵּב עָם
When disturbances disturbed Israel, when the people offered themselves willingly
(Haftorah Parashas Beshalach, Shoftim 5)

The man stood bowed before the Rebbe of Gustinin, looking utterly crushed. In tearful tones he told the Rebbe that his business had failed and he was forced to declare bankruptcy. "I am saddled with terrible debts which I am unable to pay," he sighed deeply.

The Rebbe tried to comfort him. When he rose to leave, he opened his satchel and withdrew a sum of money for his *pidyon*.

The Rebbe pushed it away. "I cannot accept this money," he said. "The prophetess Devorah, in her poetic song, said, 'When disturbances disturbed Israel, when the people offered themselves willingly.' The Hebrew, *bifroa peraos* can also be said to come from a similar root with a different meaning, *lifroa* in the sense of paying debts. We can interpret the verse in this way: before volunteering, before giving charity, one must first pay off his personal debts. When your own situation has improved, then I will accept your *pidyon* donation."

In contrast to the generosity of those who want to give, but cannot, is the stinginess of those who can give, but plead poverty. The following tale was told about the Gaon of Vilna.

The Gaon once went among the congregation to collect money for charitable causes and came to the home of one of the city's wealthier Jews. When that man heard why R' Eliyahu had come he asked, "Tell me, please, honored rabbi, if I am beset by heavy debts, which exceed the value of my own possessions and assets, am I permitted to give charity from borrowed money?"

Before the Gaon had time to reply, the local tailor entered the room bearing an expensive suit which he had just completed for the man. The Gaon looked at the suit and pointedly asked, "If what you just said is true, how were you able to afford a suit from money which was not really yours?"

"But I have not paid for it yet," explained the rich man. "I have credit with the tailor."

R' Eliyahu nodded wisely and said, "Now I understand what is written in *Yirmiyahu 9:5* 'Your dwelling is in the midst of deceit, in deceit did they refuse to acknowledge Me.' All of your dealings are crooked and for your own purposes you pile deceit on top of deceit! But if this is true, why does the verse say, 'In deceit did they refuse to acknowledge Me'? Now I understand why. Where charity is concerned, you and your like suddenly become men of truth, self-righteous people, guided only by justice. This prevents you from giving even a little money to charity!"

The Rabbi in Prison

לִבִּי לְחוֹקְקֵי יִשְׂרָאֵל הַמִּתְנַדְּבִים... בָּרְכוּ ה׳
My heart is towards the governors of Israel... bless Hashem
(Haftorah Parashas Beshalach, Shoftim 5)

R' Yitzchak Isaac Chaver, rabbi of Volkovisk, had just arrived in town. He found all the townspeople prostrated by grief and weeping.

"What is the matter? What tragedy has visited this city?" he asked in alarm.

He learned that a group of the community's young boys had just been seized by the police. They were to be transfered to distant army barracks. Twenty-five years of army duty lay before them. Twenty-five years in which they would forget all vestiges of Judaism. What a tragedy! What a misfortune! And there was nothing that could be done to save them!

"And yet, we must do whatever we can, whatever is still left in our power," the rabbi said emphatically. "Then we must put our trust in *Hashem.*"

R' Yitzchak Isaac knew that he could perform no miracles. But, there was something that he could do. After disguising himself as a peasant, he went outside and began weaving drunkenly through the streets, disturbing the pedestrians and making a scene.

The police soon caught up with him and demanded to see his papers.

"Papersh? Whatsh papersh?" he asked drunkenly.

The police decided to lock him up for the night. He was taken to jail. And this is exactly where he had wanted to go. Here he would have contact with the imprisoned Jewish youths; he would be able to speak to them before they were sent far away to the army.

R' Yitzchak Isaac was thrown into a cell. The heavy iron door clanged shut and the key turned in the lock. When the police were out of earshot, he got up and went over to the group of huddled, weeping figures.

"Psssst!' he whispered to them to catch their attention. "Don't think that I am a drunken peasant. I am really the rabbi of Volkovitzk."

The boys looked at him in amazement. A ministering angel had come to them, after all! They looked up to him with hope flickering in their tear-stained faces. The rabbi sat down among them and began talking to them in strengthening, invigorating words. "I must warn you that the exile that lies before you is long and harsh. But you must be brave and steadfast. You must try your utmost to keep the commandments of the Torah, as difficult as it will be. Be especially careful," he whispered to the boys who hung on his every word, "not to put anything forbidden into your mouth. And keep the Name of *Hashem* forever on your lips and in your heart, even if you are beaten and tortured."

The boys formed a tight circle around the venerable old man and he began telling them about the Ten Martyrs of the Roman Era, the Sages who had sacrificed their lives for *Hashem*'s Name. He told them about the brave Chanah and her seven sons who had sacrificed themselves rather than submit to idolatry.

They sat up awake all that night; the rabbi encouraged them and the boys eagerly drank in every precious word, storing it away in their memories for the difficult years to come.

Morning dawned. Soon the prison wardens would come. There were only a few minutes left. R' Yitzchak Isaac arose, scanned them with his all-embracing look, and said his last words:

"My precious lambs! I must leave you now. I am due for a heavy beating for having entered under false pretense. Worse lies ahead of you. You are embarking on a road fraught with trials and tribulations. I don't know if I will live long enough to see you return. But, we will surely meet again in the World of Eternal Truth. May it be the Divine Will, my precious flock," he concluded, tears rolling down his cheeks, "that you not disgrace me before the heavenly hosts."

The rabbi was then led away, leaving the group of boys behind him, weeping, but greatly fortified in spirit.

The following years proved indeed that those boys, who had been privileged to hear R' Yitchak Isaac Chaver's words, truly did withstand the bitter tests of time!

Letters to Chasyah

גְּדוֹלִים חִקְרֵי לֵב

There were great resolves of heart

(Haftorah Parashas Beshalach, Shoftim 5)

The brilliant and renowned R' Chaim of Volozhin had a daughter, Chasyah, whom he loved dearly. After she married and moved to Lida, he kept up a flowing correspondence with her.

Mail was not always reliable in those days and when R' Chaim learned that someone was going to Lida, he hastened to pen a letter to his daughter Chasyah. He gave it to the man, asking him to kindly deliver it in person.

The man went back to his lodgings, packed and was about to leave by coach for Lida when a messenger came running up to him. "I am sent by R' Chaim," he explained breathlessly. "He asked me to take back the first letter and to give you this one instead." The transfer of letters took place and the man rode to Lida.

People were somewhat surprised. This was unlike R' Chaim. Most puzzled of all was R' Yitzchak, son of R' Chaim and brother to Chasyah. He did not forget this strange incident.

Some time later, Chasyah herself came to Volozhin to visit her family. R' Yitzchak seized the opportunity to ask her what her father had written in his last letter. He was still bothered by the sudden exchange of letters.

When Chasyah told him about the contents of the letter, he was more surprised than ever. It was identical to the first letter that his father had written. He knew, because he had been looking over his father's shoulder at the time. What had prompted R' Chaim to write a second letter which was identical to the first?

The riddle was soon solved in the course of their conversation. Chasyah innocently began telling her brother about a story that had taken place in Lida and had been the talk of the town. A problem had arisen in the court of the famous R' Elimelech with the writing of a divorce. They had puzzled over the proper spelling of the wife's name which happened to be Chasyah. Knowing that R' Chaim's daughter who lived in Lida was also called Chasyah, R' Elimelech had sent a messenger to her to inquire exactly how her name was written in the letters which R' Chaim wrote to her.

The son now understood his father's great caution and precision. R' Chaim had most likely heard of the divorce case in Lida. In his first letter, he had apparently addressed his daughter in an endearing or inexact form of her name. But, after he had given it to the man to deliver, he suddenly remembered that he should have spelled her name properly. He felt that some misunderstanding or error might arise from such carelessness. He had therefore recalled the first letter and replaced it with a second one, identical in all but the spelling of her name. That proper spelling was to be a guide for the *beis din* of Lida.

The Elderly Charity Collector

וְאֹהֲבָיו כְּצֵאת הַשֶּׁמֶשׁ בִּגְבֻרָתוֹ

And His beloved ones are like the sun at its zenith
(Haftorah Parashas Beshalach, Shoftim 5)

They are humiliated but do not humiliate in return. They hear themselves disgraced but do not speak up... Of such is it said: 'And His beloved ones are like the sun at its zenith.'

(Tractate Shabbos 88b)

R' Nachum of Horodna had many charitable causes which he supported by going out and collecting money. One time he knocked at the door of a lawyer who had long since abandoned Jewish *mitzvah*-observance and was estranged from everything Jewish. He was a coarse, vulgar person. Small wonder then, that when he opened his door to see R' Nachum standing there, he poured his wrath upon the innocent and worthy Jew. "Who appointed you as a charity treasurer?" he growled at him. "What right do you have to ask people for money? You are nothing but a thief! I will not give you a penny. Go away and don't bother trying to extort any money from me again!"

R' Nachum did not bother to defend himself. He turned around and walked away.

Time passed and the lawyer became embroiled in some nasty business. He was taken to court. In desperation, he hired the best lawyers he knew and slipped well-placed bribes left and right, knowing that if he were convicted, he would be severely punished. However, despite all of his efforts, he spent all of his money and, nevertheless, was sentenced to two years in prison.

R' Nachum of Horodna found out about the sentence and went to the lawyer's home. There he found the lawyer's wife in deep depression. She wept openly before the kindly rabbi and said, "I am as good as a widow for the next two years. My husband has left me no money; the trial ate up all of our funds. I don't know what we will do, how my children and I will survive. We are penniless. We will starve to death!"

"Don't worry!" R' Nachum hastened to console her. "*Hashem* will surely help you. *Hashem*'s salvation can come in the twinkling of an eye. Tell me, though, how much money do you need each week?"

She sighed, "My weekly budget is twenty rubles."

The rabbi took out his wallet and laid twenty rubles

down on the table. "Here, this will tide you over the first week. Consider it as a loan. And now you must continue living as before, not stinting, but keeping up your usual standard of living. Do not move away or sell any furniture. Leave everything, just as it is, and I will keep on providing you with your weekly twenty rubles."

For the next two years R' Nachum kept his word. Week after week, he would deposit the twenty rubles on the table, coming and going as quietly as possible.

Those two years were very long and difficult for the imprisoned lawyer. When he was finally released, he stood on the street and wondered what to do.

"Shall I go to my home?" he thought. "Who knows if my family still lives there. They must surely have moved to more modest quarters, sold the furniture, changed their entire life style. Where will I find them? And in what state?"

He finally decided to return to his home. There, he found everything exactly as it had been. All the furniture was intact and his wife and children looked well, as if nothing had happened.

"How have you passed these two years?" he asked, looking around the house in wide-eyed astonishment. "Where did you find money for food and clothing? What did you live on?"

His wife smiled at him and said, "Do you remember the old Jew who once came here collecting for charity? His name is R' Nachum. He is the one who supported us during your two years of absence. Each week he would bring me twenty rubles. We did not even have to sell anything. If not for him, I don't know what I would have done."

"The charity collector, you said? The man whom I

chased away from our door so rudely?" Without even waiting for her answer, he rushed out of the house and headed for R' Nachum's.

He burst in and threw himself at R' Nachum's feet. "Rebbe, how can you forgive me for treating you so badly, for embarrassing you? How can I begin to thank you for the tremendous help you gave to my family? I have no words to express my overwhelming feelings. Let me promise you, here and now, that as soon as I begin earning some money I will return every last penny that you gave me, and much more besides, so that you can continue to do your charitable work!"

The lawyer became a changed man. He slowly began practicing all Jewish laws and customs and gave generously to every charitable cause.

פָּרָשַׁת יִתְרוֹ

Parashas Yisro

About Deeds and Thoughts

עַתָּה יָדַעְתִּי כִּי בַדָּבָר אֲשֶׁר זָדוּ עֲלֵיהֶם

Now I know... that in the thing which they plotted against them (18:11)

The wealthy minister hated all Jews, but one particular neighbor more than the rest. This Jew was a saintly man who spent all of his days in Torah study and prayer, leaving his house early each morning and returning late at night. The very sight of this pure man, wrapped up in his *tallis*, heading for the *beis medrash* day in, day out, summer and winter, irritated the minister. The sound of the man's footsteps haunted him.

Aware of the Jew's regular habits, the gentile thought of a way to kill him while making his death look like an accident. One night, after the Jew had returned from his study, the rich man sent a servant out to dig a deep ditch in the road. The Jew, who left his home each morning while it was still dark, would not see the ditch, fall in and break his neck.

But that evening, the good Jew had a distinguished guest. They dined together and dallied over the table, 'talking in learning' until late at night. The good Jew went to bed much later than usual and overslept the next morning. By the time he left his house for the *beis medrash*, it was already light. When he came to the ditch, he skirted it and continued innocently on his way.

The minister was certain that the Jew had met his death that morning. He ran outside to examine the ditch. To his surprise, there was the Jew on his way to the *beis medrash*. He ran up to him and asked, "Why are you so late this morning?"

The good man told him about his guest with whom he had spent the last evening and how he had gone to sleep so late. The minister could not hide his wonder at his enemy's narrow escape and cried out, "Praised be the G-d of the Jews Who devises all kinds of ways to rescue His devoted sons!"

The Chozeh of Lublin told this tale in illustrating the verse, "Praise Hashem, all you nations... for His kindness is mighty."

"We Jews," said the Chozeh, "do not begin to realize all of the miracles that take place, day by day. The gentiles, however, who ceaselessly plot and scheme against us, they are the ones who know how many are the miracles which take place each and every day, to protect Jews from all harm!"

This verse has an additional explanation.

Yisro said, "Now I know that *Hashem* is indeed mightier than all other gods... that in the thing which they plotted against them." Yisro, who was Pharaoh's advisor, knew of all the evil schemes which the Egyptians constantly planned against the Jews. He knew of the ones that were never carried out, but only planned and thwarted through divine interference, as well as those which were carried out.

When the Egyptians were punished, Yisro saw that they suffered not only for the actual evil which they did, but even for the evil which they had planned but did not execute; for their thoughts as well as their deeds.

Spoon to Mouth

וַיָּבֹא אַהֲרֹן וְכֹל זִקְנֵי יִשְׂרָאֵל לֶאֱכָל לֶחֶם... לִפְנֵי הָאֱלֹהִים
And Aharon and all the Elders of Israel came to eat bread... before Elokim (18:12)

We learn from here that one who partakes from a meal at which Torah scholars are present can be said to have basked in the light of the Shechinah

(Rashi)

Because he feared the persecutions of the Russian government, R' Yisrael of Ruzhin fled to Austria. The Russians, however, first requested, and then demanded, of the Austrians that the Rebbe be extradited and sent back to Russia.

The Jews used all of their influence to prevent such a terrible thing. They needed character recommendations from Austrian rabbis to bring to high-placed officials in Vienna testifying to R' Yisrael's honesty and good name.

Before setting out for the Austrian capital, several of R' Yisrael's chasidim came to R' Dov Ber Meislish, rabbi of Cracow, for a letter of reference.

R' Dov Ber had never met R' Yisrael.

"What is the Rebbe like? Why do people regard him as a great man?" R' Dov Ber asked the chasidim.

One of them replied: "His greatness is evident in the fact that he is capable of exceptional self-control."

"How is this expressed?" R' Dov Ber asked.

The chasid answered, "The Ruzhiner Rebbe never bends his head to a spoon during mealtime."

This statement was greeted by a burst of laughter. Was

this the measure of a great man, his eating habits?

"I can do the same," said the rabbi. It was lunchtime then. R' Dov Ber washed his hands and sat down to eat. Everyone looked as he lifted his soup spoon to his mouth.

At the critical moment, just as the spoon was about to reach its destination, the rabbi inclined his head slightly toward the spoon.

"Try again!" his family encouraged him.

"That is unnecessary," Reb Dov Ber admitted. Turning to the chasidim, he said, "You were right. That is truly a remarkable feat of self-control." And he wrote out a letter of recommendation at once.

The Sick Student

וְהוֹדַעְתָּ לָהֶם אֶת הַדֶּרֶךְ יֵלְכוּ

And you shall show them the way they are to follow (18:20)

This refers to bikur cholim

(Bava Kama 100a)

One of R' Akiva's students had become ill. He took to his bed, but no one came to visit him; no one inquired about his health or offered any help.

R' Akiva had twenty-four thousand disciples, yet he noticed the absence of this one student. He asked after him and learned that he was ill. R' Akiva went to visit him.

He found the sick student lying in bed, his face pale, his lips parched with fever and thirst, his breathing labored. He was very ill indeed.

R' Akiva looked around the room and saw signs of gross neglect. He opened the windows, dusted, swept, brushed away cobwebs and made the room presentable.

As soon as the room was neat and clean, R' Akiva turned his attention to the patient. He seemed much better already! In a grateful tone, he turned to R' Akiva and said, "Rebbe, you have revived me! Had you not come to visit me at this crucial time, I don't know if I would have lived!"

R' Akiva reassured him that he would soon get better, wished him a "*Refuah sheleimah*" and left the house. He immediately went to the *beis midrash* and said to his students, "Let me tell you that whoever does not visit a sick man is responsible, as it were, for his death. If the sick man does not receive help, his condition gets worse and worse and he is liable to die. But, if you visit the sick man, help him and bring him food and drink, he gets somewhat better and his recovery is quick to follow."

(Adapted from Tractate *Nedarim 40a*)

He Did Not Sit

אַנְשֵׁי אֱמֶת
Men of truth (18:21)

Despite his advanced age, R' Avraham of Cheknow was determined to attend an important convention that was to deal with vital Jewish matters. His family tried their best to dissuade him.

"You are so weak. The trip will ruin your health, father," his sons warned.

R' Avraham was adamant. "Do you think," he asked, "that I intend to sit out the entire convention?" He meant, of course, that he did not intend to stay for all the speeches, but, simply, to show his face and then return home.

His family soon realized that R' Avraham was not to be deterred and allowed him to go despite their fears. Those who were present at the convention noted, with surprise, that he refused to sit, even though he was offered a seat time and again. Why? Because he had inadvertently uttered the words, "I do not intend to sit out the entire convention." This prevented his conscience from letting him sit even for a moment!

The Soup Can Wait

וְשָׁפְטוּ אֶת הָעָם בְּכָל עֵת

And they will judge the people at all times (18:22)

The wind howled; the rain came down in torrents. It was weather for ducks, not for people. There was hardly anyone out and those who had to venture forth for some reason or other ran from one place of cover to another.

In R' Chaim Falaggi's house the maid was setting the table for lunch. The rabbi of Izmir was expected shortly and she did not want him to wait for his hot soup.

There was his step. R' Chaim entered, took off his dripping overcoat and gave it to the maid to hang up. "Brrrr!" he shivered. "It's freezing outside!" He began coughing.

"How glad I am that I made a hot soup today," the *rebbetzin* said. "That is just the thing you need for your cough. We don't want it to develop into anything worse, G-d forbid! Come, wash your hands and sit down to eat while it is still hot."

"You are so right. A bowl of steaming soup is just what I need," replied R' Chaim, going to wash his hands.

As soon as he was seated, the maid entered bearing a steaming bowl of soup which she set before him. Just as R' Chaim was lifting the first spoonful to his mouth, there was a knock at the front door. His wife rushed to answer it, not wanting her husband to get up. There stood an old woman who kept a stall in the marketplace.

"Is the rabbi home?" she asked.

"Y-yes," the *rebbetzin* hesitated, "but he has just come home for lunch. Can the matter wait? Could you come back in an hour or two?"

"Certainly," said the old woman, not wanting to disturb the rabbi from his meal. She turned around and thrust herself into the rain.

The rabbi's wife looked at her receding figure and thought to herself, "I am glad that I told her to go away. Had I told the rabbi that someone was waiting for him, he would surely have gotten up right away and spoken to her. Then his soup would have gotten cold and would not have done him any good. In his condition, he cannot afford to take any chances. Izmir needs a healthy rabbi! The woman can wait; she said so herself."

With these comforting thoughts, she returned to the table.

"Who was that at the door?" the rabbi asked, curiously.

"Oh, just some old woman from the community."

"What did she want?"

"She wanted to speak to you."

Hearing this, R' Chaim jumped up from his chair. His wife stopped him with her next words: "Don't bother. She left already. She said she would come back in an hour or two."

"An old woman came here to speak to me and you sent her away?" he asked incredulously.

"But she herself said that the matter was not urgent," his wife said, justifying herself. R' Chaim was not listening. He had already washed with the *mayim acharonim* and was now saying the *birkas hamazon*. As soon as he had finished, he stood up and put on his soaking overcoat and hat.

"Come!" he called out to his *shammash*. "We are going to the peddler-woman's home.

"But it is so stormy outside," said the *shammash*. He tried to dissuade the rabbi, "And you have a cough and sore throat."

"Never mind! We must go at once!" said R' Chaim, halfway out the door.

A fearsome wind blasted them, almost throwing them off balance. R' Chaim walked with sure steps, battling the fierce wind; his attendant plodded reluctantly behind. They walked thus through the almost deserted streets, hugging their coats to their bodies.

Finally they reached the marketplace. Even this was almost deserted. Only a few isolated customers, looking for bargains, were fingering the sodden fruits and

vegetables. The two threaded their way between puddles and mud until they finally reached the rickety door of the elderly woman.

R' Chaim knocked on the paint-chipped door. He could hear heavy steps approaching. Then the door opened and the woman peered out at him.

"Rabbi!" she cried out in alarm, seeing who stood at her doorstep. "Why did you trouble yourself to come here on this freezing day? I was about to come to you myself in about an hour!"

"Forgive me, good woman, for having sent you away from my house. It was done without my knowledge, for had I known that you were waiting in the doorway, I would surely have gotten up to talk to you!"

Standing there, bewildered, the woman managed to reply, "Yes, of course I forgive you. But it was hardly necessary for you to come all the way here! Really!"

At home the *rebbetzin* sat in her warm house, looking disconsolately out the window. She could see the wind battling with the trees and the rain still falling steadily. Her conscience bothered her for having sent the old woman away. Still, she did not understand what harm she had done. Her thoughts had been only about her coughing husband. It was his interest that she had had at heart. How sorry she was that he had to make this long trip on foot in this weather.

Suddenly she spied him from afar. She rushed to the door to greet him.

After the rabbi had removed his sopping overcoat and was seated by the crackling fire, nursing a cup of tea in his hands, his wife dared to ask, "Why were you so upset that I sent the old woman away? As you know, I had very valid reasons for doing so."

The rabbi sat back and said, "Let me tell you a story which is brought in *Mechilta* on *Parashas Mishpatim*:

R' Shimon and R' Yishmael were two of the Ten Martyrs of the Roman period. When they were taken out to be executed, the first turned to the second and said, "I have examined my deeds thoroughly but cannot find any sin for which I might be punished now."

R' Yishamel replied, "Did it ever happen to you that a person came to your house to clarify a law or ask a *halachic* question and you detained him while you finished a drink, tied your shoe or put on your cloak?' He continued, "The Torah states: 'If you shall oppress...' This prohibition concerns any form of suffering, from great to small, including the postponing of the judge's pronouncement of a sentence. In this case, every small delay is considered painful for those involved!'

When R' Shimon heard this he said, "You have comforted me."

"Do you see now," R' Chaim turned to his wife, "why I was so upset? I prefer to eat cold meals on wintry days for the rest of my life, as long as I am not considered a judge who oppresses the members of his congregation!"

The Special Diamond

וְאַתֶּם תִּהְיוּ לִי מַמְלֶכֶת כֹּהֲנִים וְגוֹי קָדוֹשׁ

And you shall be unto Me a kingdom of priests and a holy nation (19:6)

The wealthy diamond merchant, a devoted follower and supporter of the Lubavitcher Rebbe, once visited the Rebbe and was shown into his room. They talked about this and that until the conversation turned to the topic of simple folk. The Rebbe had a special love of simple Jews and always praised them highly.

The rich man could not contain his disapproval and said, "Why is the Rebbe so impressed by common folk? They are, after all, unlearned."

"But they have many valuable redeeming traits," said the Rebbe.

"Well I for one do not see that!" replied the rich merchant in a huff.

The Rebbe did not try to convince him but changed the topic. Soon the conversation took a turn to business matters. The Rebbe asked his guest, "Do you have any of your famous gems with you here?"

The merchant said, "Yes, I do, but I cannot show them to you yet. The sun is shining right into the room and would spoil the effect of the gems."

A few minutes later the sun had changed its angle and was no longer shining directly into the room.

Beaming, the merchant now took out a small packet. In it was a piece of rice paper folded many times over. Carefully and lovingly he peeled off the layers of tissue paper, revealing several gleaming jewels. Pointing to one of them, he said, "This is a real beauty, a rare gem."

"Really? I don't see anything extraordinary about that stone?" the Rebbe noted.

"Ah! But one must be an expert to see and appreciate diamonds!"

The Rebbe retorted, "And there are gems of souls amongst our people. But one must be an 'expert' in human nature to see and appreciate these jewels!"

When the Heart Was Frozen

וַיֶּחֱרַד כָּל הָעָם
And all the people trembled (19:16)

Once, the Baal Shem Tov passed by a river that had frozen over. "Look there!" he said. The *talmidim* looked at the frozen surface of the river and saw that gentiles had carved out the sign of a cross on the ice. The Baal Shem Tov turned to his students and said, "As you know, there is nothing like the flowing water of a river for purification. But when the river is frozen one can even carve a cross on it.

The same holds true for the human heart. A person must serve his Creator with a burning, fervent heart, never with cold indifference. For see the effects of coldness and frost."

The Rabbi and the Butcher

כַּבֵּד אֶת אָבִיךָ וְאֶת אִמֶּךָ
Honor your father and your mother (20:18)

R' Yehoshua ben Eilam, one of the great sages of his generation, once had a puzzling dream: he was told to rejoice because he was to sit in *Gan Eden* alongside Nanas the butcher.

He awoke with his heart beating and his mind buzzing. "How can that be?" he wondered sadly. "From the day I was born I feared *Hashem* and carefully kept all of the commandments. I study Torah devotedly; I have made that the labor of my life. I even have eighty worthy disciples to prove it. I am careful not to walk more than four cubits without *tefillin*! How can my deeds be compared to those of a coarse butcher who certainly does not have the time or the head to study Torah? What can be so extraordinary about a simple butcher?

He was so disturbed by these thoughts that he gathered his eighty disciples and said to them, "I cannot enter the *beis midrash* and teach you until I find out who this butcher Nanas is, and what are his worthy deeds which are equal to my learning."

He rose and followed by his disciples, went to search for Nanas the butcher. He went from city to city, asking if a butcher named Nanas lived there. And wherever he went, the townspeople wondered what could a great scholar possibly have to say to a butcher.

Finally, they located him. R' Yehoshua asked the townspeople if there was anything special about Nanas. They shook their heads. "You had better see him yourself," they suggested and sent messengers to fetch him.

They found him in his shop. "R' Yehoshua ben Eilam has come here asking for you," they informed him.

The butcher was shocked. "Who am I that R' Yehoshua should be looking for me?"

"Come with us and see for yourself," they said.

"You are making fun of me!" he retorted angrily. "This is some nasty trick. I refuse to go with you."

The messengers shrugged their shoulders and returned

to R' Yehoshua. "He refuses to come with us," they said.

"But I must see him!" R' Yehoshua said. "I will not sit down until I see him!" And off he went to the butcher.

When Nanas saw R' Yehoshua, the sage of the generation, standing on his threshold, he turned pale. He rushed up to the rabbi and fell at his feet, crying, "What special occasion brings such a great man as you to my doorstep?" He trembled with fear.

"I must speak to you," said R' Yehoshua. "Tell me, what do you do besides your work?"

Nanas replied, "I don't really have time for anything. You see, I have elderly parents who are feeble and helpless. They cannot even stand up. I must do everything for them: feed, dress and bathe them, all by myself."

R' Yehoshua kissed him on the forehead and said, "Fortunate are you, my son, and blessed is your portion. Now I understand the meaning of my dream. How glad I am that I am to be privileged to be together with you in the World to Come!"

(Adapted from *Sefer Hamaasiyos*)

The Merchant's Suggestion

לֹא תִגְנֹב
You shall not steal (20:13)

The inn teemed with people. There was so much activity that no one paid any attention to the visitor who had just come in and was now restlessly pacing the floor, to and fro, his face knotted up with anxiety.

The man, a fabulously wealthy merchant, kept on glancing at a leather money pouch at his side which, by its size and apparent weight, seemed to contain a considerable sum.

Indeed, five hundred gold coins rested in the rich merchant's pouch. This money was the cause of his anxiety. It was the fruit of his business trips. But such a fat money pouch was sure to attract thieves who could turn him into a pauper overnight.

All the other guests at the inn seemed preoccupied with their own affairs; no one gave him as much as a second glance. All — except for one man, the innkeeper himself, who was watching him from the corner of his eye. From the moment the merchant had come in, he had studied him.

The guest's bulging pouch and his distinguished air had attracted the attention of the innkeeper, who had an eye for rich men. Nor had the man's evident uneasiness escaped the innkeeper's sharp eye either.

While the innkeeper watched stealthily, he noticed the man's expression suddenly change. A mysterious smile spread over his face; he stopped his pacing and hurried outside, money pouch in hand. The innkeeper slipped out and followed silently behind.

After a few minutes of walking, the rich merchant reached a wood. Here, he stopped and examined the area.

The inkeeper, afraid of being detected, climbed up a tree. From there he could see everything happening below and not be seen himself.

Peering down, he saw his wealthy guest take up a pointed iron bar and begin digging. The man worked diligently until he had dug a small pit.

The merchant eagerly took his money pouch and buried it in the hole he had just dug. He filled it with earth and patted it over smoothly. He straightened up, sighed with satisfaction and stretched, realizing, all of a sudden, how tired he was. He sat down by a tree to rest for a while. After he felt refreshed, he got up and continued on his way.

The innkeeper in the tree waited until the man was at a distance. Then, he climbed down and claimed the booty. He dug up the earth easily and seized the money pouch. With trembling hands, he lifted it out of the hole and ran back to the inn.

The businessman continued on his travels with a light heart, certain that his five hundred coins were safe.

Time passed and the merchant returned to retrieve his buried fortune. With a sure step he approached his hiding place and began digging, casting up layer after layer of earth. He dug and dug, expecting to come across his pouch. Where was it? Could he have hidden it so deeply? He was sure that he had made no mistake about the exact location. A deathly pallor crept over his features when it finally dawned upon him that his treasure was gone. Someone had taken it! Some evil person had stolen it! He stood there, dumbfounded, for a few minutes, unable to move. But then he began to think cooly.

His immediate suspicion fell upon the innkeeper who had not made a favorable impression on him. There had been something snoopy and underhanded about his manner, as he recalled.

Aside from wealth, this businessman was also blessed with a clever mind. He quickly came up with a plan.

He headed for the inn and approached the innkeeper. Talking in a low voice, he asked to speak to him privately.

"I would like a word with you," he began. The innkeeper tried not to show his inner agitation. But, seeing the guest's calm expression, he knew, at once, that he had nothing to fear. He listened attentively.

"My friend, I have heard that you are a smart man. That is why I have come to you for advice on a very important matter."

The innkeeper felt his curiosity rise and the guest continued. "This must be kept secret, you realize. The matter is this: as you can see, I am a businessman and must carry around a lot of cash on my person. This time I have two purses full. One of them contains five hundred coins while the other has eight hundred."

The innkeeper's eyes widened greedily.

The businessman lowered his voice to a whisper. "I already hid one of them in a secret place and am debating what to do with the other which contains an even larger fortune. What do you think?"

"Are you thinking of entrusting it to a person?" the innkeeper asked. "Do you have anyone trustworthy enough? You are a stranger here. Whom do you know?"

He paused, then said, "If you were to listen to me, you would take that purse and hide it exactly where you put the other one. That is the safest thing. That's what I would do in your place."

Now the merchant had no doubt that he was the thief. He pretended to weigh the idea in his mind, then said, "I think you are right. Thank you for your advice."

He left the inn. Now the innkeeper had to move quickly. For he thought that when the merchant went to hide the second purse in the same place as the first he would discover that it was gone and he would not put the second one there. The innkeeper rushed off to the forest to rebury the money pouch containing the five hundred coins.

He put it back, considering it a good investment, for soon he would be richer by another eight hundred coins! He gloated at the prospect.

Shortly after the innkeeper had left the woods, the merchant arrived. Then he dug up the hole once more, not to place a second pouch of coins there but to retrieve the first, and only, one.

And when he had it safe in his hands, he lifted his eyes to Heaven and movingly said, "Praised be He Who restores lost property to its owner."

The Test

לְבַעֲבוּר נַסּוֹת אֶתְכֶם
In order to test you (20:17)

R' Menachem Mendel of Riminov respected his *shammash* greatly; he was always praising Reb Hirsch to the skies. Many of the chasidim, however, resented some of the things Reb Hirsch did, such as the way he prayed. Reb Hirsch would close his eyes tightly and weave back and forth in fervent ecstacy. The chasidim felt that it was not genuine. Worse, it was a poor imitation of the Rebbe's devotion during prayer. They decided to put Reb Hirsch to the test and expose his falseness, once and for all.

It was Reb Hirsh's custom to stand by the pot-bellied iron stove that stood in the *beis medrash*. When his enthusiasm reached its peak, he would lean his entire body against it. During prayer, the stove was generally not lit.

The chasidim decided that they would light up the stove just before Reb Hirsch came to pray. He would not notice anything as it took time to warm up. But, by the time he was at his peak fervor, it would be glowing hot!

They carried out their plan. Reb Hirsch did not notice anything unusual and began praying as always. Meanwhile, the stove became hotter and hotter and still Reb Hirsh did not notice anything. When he reached his climax of adherence and concentration, he leaned his head and arm on the stove, as he always did. He did not snatch them away because of the heat. He seemed impervious to it, totally unconscious.

Reb Hirsch's face and hands were being severely burned. And still he continued on, oblivious of all pain.

Only then did the chasidim realize that the esteem the Rebbe had always shown for Reb Hirsch was truly well deserved.

"I Am Ashamed!"

וּבַעֲבוּר תִּהְיֶה יִרְאָתוֹ עַל פְּנֵיכֶם

And so that His fear be upon your faces (20:17)

"His fear be upon your faces" — this refers to shame.

(Tractate *Nedarim 20b*)

One year on *erev Yom Kippur* R' Naftali of Ropshitz entered his room right after the last meal before the fast and did not come out for the *Kol Nidre* prayer.

The chasidim waited and waited. Soon the sun would

set. But the Rebbe did not appear. They looked at R' Eliezer, the Rebbe's son, as if to indicate that he should tell his father to come out. R' Eliezer knocked at the door of his father's room and entered. He found the Rebbe in tears, crying like a baby.

"Father!" he said with awe and humility in his voice. "Why are you not coming out. The people are waiting for you to begin *Kol Nidre.*"

"Oh, my son. Alas! I am too embarrassed to enter the *beis medrash*. For a whole year, each and every day, I have been promising myself that I would do *teshuvah* and improve my actions. But the year has already passed and I have not done so yet! When *Rosh Hashanah* came, I promised myself that I would repent during the Ten Days of Repentance. And now, here it is, the eve of *Yom Kippur*, and I still have not repented!" He burst into a fresh torrent of tears.

"But father! I am certain that now, during *Kol Nidre*, you will repent wholeheartedly," the son reassured him.

When he heard these words, R' Naftali relaxed. Together with his son he entered the *beis medrash*, confident that now he would truly repent.

Everything is Ownerless

וּלְסַעֲדָהּ בְּמִשְׁפָּט וּבִצְדָקָה
To uphold it through justice and through righteousness
(Haftorah Parashas Yisro, Yeshayah 9)

It was past midnight. The entire city was already sleeping, or so the thief thought when he sneaked into the cellar of R' Nosson Adler, the 'Great Eagle', and came out with a bundle of firewood.

R' Nosson Adler, the brilliant Talmudist and kabbalist, did not devote much of the night hours to sleeping; he was wide awake. He did not hear the burglar enter, but did see him leave, carrying the bundle of sticks.

"Hefker! Hefker!" he cried out in the stillness of the night. What he meant to say was that he was laying aside all claim to the firewood; it was no longer his property and therefore was not stolen goods.

Since he was not certain that his meaning was clear to the thief, he ran out and chased after him in order to explain himself. He soon overtook the man and his bulky, unwieldy bundle.

The thief, misunderstanding his intention, stopped, caught red-handed. He shivered with fear and waited for the curses that would be heaped upon his head. Instead, R' Nosson said, "You are lucky, my friend, that I was sitting by the window just when you chose to take the wood. Had I not been there to see or had it been anyone else, you would have been guilty of robbery! And that is an act forbidden by the Torah!!!"

The thief had certainly not expected words of this kind! In his confusion, he dropped his bundle. It fell and broke apart, the sticks scattering in all directions.

Before the thief could even utter a word, R' Nosson was down on the ground, gathering up the sticks. He handed the bundle to the stunned thief, saying, "I am truly sorry that I did not help you carry this heavy, bulky load. That is another *mitzvah* in the Torah. It is familiar to everyone but somehow, it slipped my mind just now."

The next morning, when R' Nosson Adler thought the matter over, he decided to waive claim to everything he owned lest some other thief, less lucky than that one, would come and be guilty of stealing. He hung a sign on his front door. It read:

"Everything in this house is *hefker*, ownerless."

"From Whence Shall Come My Help?"

וּלְסַעֲדָהּ בְּמִשְׁפָּט וּבִצְדָקָה

To uphold it through justice and through righteousness

(Haftorah Parashas Yisro, Yeshayah 9)

In Russia, a law had been enacted that distillers and brewers of beer and whiskey had to pay a tax according to their sales. To determine the sales the government installed meters which measured the liquor which was drawn off.

Reb Shmuel, who owned a large distillery was an honest man; he made no attempt to tamper with the meter. Among his workers, however, was a gentile who was not trustworthy. He had found a small hole at the bottom of one of the large barrels from which he could siphon off whiskey for his own use without the owner or the government being any the wiser.

He might have continued at his petty thievery indefinitely had not another worker noticed it. He threatened to report him to Reb Shmuel, the owner, unless the thief made him a partner. Now two people were taking liquor without reporting it.

This would also not have caused any problems had not the two begun quarreling over the fairness of the distribution. Each accused the other of cheating. Finally, one of them went to the authorities. The police swooped down on the distillery and arrested the other. He claimed to be innocent. "The owner, our employer, made us steal, so that he could bypass the meter and gain extra profits for himself," he pleaded.

The police believed the man and freed him, but they arrested Reb Shmuel instead! They charged him with tax evasion, a very serious offense in Russia.

The punishment was a high fine, long exile in a hard labor camp in Siberia and confiscation of the accused's property. Reb Shmuel's family made every effort to prove his innocence and honesty. They finally succeeded in having him released on high bail until his trial.

When Reb Shmuel was released he traveled to the Lubavitcher Rebbe to ask for advice and help.

A long line of people stood outside the Rebbe's chamber. The *gabbai* told the new arrival that he would have to wait several days before his turn came to speak to the Rebbe.

"Several days?" he faltered, his hopes were dashed to the ground. Every moment was crucial. He had to prepare his case before the trial! In his desperation, he poured out his woeful tale to the *gabbai*. The latter could not help being moved and promised to let Reb Shmuel in the next day. All that night Reb Shmuel sat in the *beis medrash* praying, reciting *Tehillim* and weeping profusely. His broken and hoarse voice filled the room.

When his turn came he was a broken, crushed person. He could hardly even speak. Slowly, the Rebbe drew out the sad story of the case against him. He described the probable consequences of his trial. "I am dealing with dishonest workers who will lie and defame me. How can I possibly fight that, I, who have always been an honest, upright person?" He sighed deeply. "'From whence shall come my help?'" he quoted the words of *Tehillim,* so familiar to his lips.

When he fell silent, the Rebbe spoke, "Listen to me: when you meet up with a Jew who uses that very same verse, 'From whence shall come my help,' help him to the best of your ability. When you succeed in helping him, you will be helped in turn."

Reb Shmuel felt his spirits lift. He set out for home, a different man from the one who had come, confident that *Hashem* would come to his aid.

When he reached his town he was given a hero's welcome. People had not seen him since he had been imprisoned. After all his friends and acquaintances had greeted him and wished him well in his forthcoming trial, they told him the latest news. It concerned his friend, Reb Chaim.

Reb Chaim, an upright, decent person, like Reb Shmuel himself, had a large family which he supported by running a restaurant which stood near the river that ran by the town. Reb Chaim had just suffered a terrible misfortune. His house and restaurant had burned down to the ground. How would he ever get back on his feet? How would he support his family? Where would he live? He did not even have a roof over his head!

Reb Shmuel became very upset. He ran to seek Reb Chaim and offer him his consolation. He went towards the spot where, only a few days before, Reb Chaim's house and restaurant had stood. From a distance he was already able to smell the acrid traces of smoke hovering in the air. When he approached, he saw Reb Chaim standing among the charred debris, the rubble of his home. His head was bent, his expression very grave.

As soon as Reb Chaim sensed his presence, he looked up and his eyes lit up. All of his personal woes were forgotten in the glad sight of his friend who had just been released from prison, even if it was only a temporary reprieve.

"Reb Shmuel! How happy I am to see you! Blessed is He Who frees the imprisoned."

It was now Reb Shmuel's turn to look depressed. His heart ached at the desolate sight. He looked all around and tried to find the right words to comfort his friend in his plight.

Finally he asked, "Reb Chaim, what sum would you need to rebuild your house and business?"

Reb Chaim raised his eyebrows. What did he mean?

Reb Shmuel waited for an answer to his question. Finally Reb Chaim quoted a price.

"I am prepared to lend you that sum," said Reb Shmuel without hesitating.

It was an enormous figure. "How can I accept such a large sum?" asked Reb Chaim, "First of all, I don't know when I will be able to pay it back. Secondly, you yourself are in trouble. You have a trial coming up soon and need the best defense money can buy. No, my dear friend, I cannot accept your kind and generous offer. Surely *Hashem* will help me! As it says in *Tehillim*, 'From whence shall come my help? My help is from *Hashem*, Creator of heaven and earth!' The Creator is also the A-mighty. He will surely come to my aid!"

The words "from whence shall come my help" struck a bell in Reb Shmuel's mind, a welcome note. For Reb

Shmuel suddenly remembered what the Rebbe had told him. "When you meet up with a Jew who uses that very same verse, help him to the best of your ability." This, he remembered, would be the key to his own salvation.

"Reb Chaim," he now begged his friend, "I absolutely insist that you take the money!"

Reb Chaim refused. Despite his difficult circumstances, faced with no roof over his head and no means of livelihood, he would not take money from his friend who would also need funds for the trial.

"Take it as a loan! You must! You cannot refuse me; it means so much to me to see you able to stand on your two feet again. As for me, *Hashem* will take care of me as well!"

After much pleading and coaxing, Reb Chaim finally agreed to accept the amount. Reb Shmuel felt as if a load had been removed from his own shoulders when he saw how relieved his good friend was. In excellent spirits he returned home to fetch the money.

Reb Chaim was moved to tears as he accepted the loan which would rehabilitate him. "Reb Shmuel," he whispered, overcome with emotion, "from the bottom of my heart, I want to wish you success in your forthcoming trial. May *Hashem* free you of the terrible charge and bring your innocence to light."

Time passed slowly for Reb Shmuel, but finally the day of the trial arrived. Reb Shmuel was led into the courtroom and shown to the defendant's bench. In the visitor's gallery, opposite the judge and jury, sat all of his friends and relatives, weeping and murmuring *Tehillim,* praying that the outcome of this trial would be for the best.

The judge pounded his gavel for attention and the trial

began. Witnesses were brought one after the other to bear testimony, among them the two workers who had falsely accused their employer. Even in the somber courtroom they persisted in their lies. "We knew about our employer's dishonesty for a long time but he threatened to dismiss us if we dared say anything," they testified.

After the witnesses for the prosecution had all testified, the prosecuting lawyer summed up the case in an oration full of hate and prejudice. "Before us," he addressed the judge and jurors, "sits an evil criminal who took advantage of his innocent workers in order to deceive the government. I demand justice in this court. I demand that the jury bring forth a verdict of 'guilty' and punish him to the full severity of the law."

Reb Shmuel now arose to say a few words of self-defense. Before he arose, he glanced at the two rows of jurors, those men upon whom his fate depended. Their faces reflected the poison which the prosecution had planted in their hearts. Reb Shmuel could already see the outcome of his trial.

Dejectedly, he arose and croaked forth a few words in his own defense, feeling them useless at this point. "I am innocent, honored jurors. I am not to blame. I am the victim of a terrible frame-up, a false libel. I have never taken a penny that was not mine; I have never cheated or deceived anyone! Believe me!"

He fell back on the bench with a thud. His head fell forward and he began weeping silently between his hands.

It was now the judge's turn to sum up the case, before allowing the jurors to retire to the judicial chambers and arrive at their verdict. It was his duty to clear up points of the law to guide them in their decision.

He said, "What remains now is to decide whom to believe — the Jew sitting before us or the two employees, who themselves admitted that they were accomplices to the crime. But before you retire to make your decision, I would like to tell you a short story."

All eyes were turned towards the judge. Everyone's curiosity was aroused. What story could possibly throw any light on this case, people wondered. He began:

A young man from an aristocratic family once set out on a long journey to seek his fortune. He traveled by train and, when he reached his destination, he suddenly discovered that the suitcase with his papers and money had been stolen. He got off the train, not knowing what to do. He did not even have his return ticket. Helplessly, he wandered around the train station all day. He did not know where to turn. His increasing hunger did not help his spirits either. No one took any notice of him in that busy terminal. When night fell, he lay down on one of the benches and slept a troubled sleep.

Life hardly looked rosier the next morning. He was almost prepared to beg for money, some food and a train ticket, when a man came over to him. It was a businessman who had just gotten off the train and had noticed the youth with the helpless, forlorn expression. His keen eye had also noticed that this was no common vagrant, but a young aristocrat who had had some misfortune. He tapped him on the shoulder and asked, "Would you like to join me for a cup of coffee? You look as though you could use one." The young man was too overcome to even reply. He merely nodded in agreement and let himself be led to a nearby restaurant. The kind businessman bought him a satisfying meal and things took on a better light. The young man disclosed what had happened to him the previous day, explaining that now he was at a loss; he did not even have the money for a return ticket. Without even hesitating, the businessman took out a few bills and went to buy him a ticket. He gave him another bill for pocket money. The young man thanked him heartily, but begged that he give him his name and address, so that he might return the money when he got home. The kind man refused. "Go and good luck to you," he said and they parted.

"Many years have passed since that day," the judge concluded. "The young man grew into an adult and turned to law. He is none other than myself, seated here before you. You must surely be wondering who that kind angel of mercy was who helped me without even knowing me. Let me tell you: it was the very man seated here in this courtroom, the accused, Reb Shmuel!"

The judge paused for effect, then continued, "I have searched for my benefactor for many years, but in vain. I wanted to repay my debt to him. As I wandered dejected in that train station, hundreds of people passed by, but ignored my plight. It was only that Jewish businessman who took an interest in me and helped me in my time of need. When he was brought to this courtroom today I suddenly recognized him. Now I ask you, do you think that a man of such noble character is capable of cheating and lying? If he insists that he is innocent of any crime, can we not take his word for it? Surely he is no liar. Surely he is no thief! Before you reach your verdict, members of the jury, I hope you take my personal character reference into account. Know who this Reb Shmuel is before coming to your decision."

The judge now bowed his head to the court clerk, who

showed the jury to their chambers. They filed out one by one. Their consultation did not take long. When they returned, their spokesman announced their verdict: "The accused is innocent of the charges."

Reb Shmuel sat upon the bench, stunned. He could hardly believe his ears. But inside, an inner voice repeated something that he had heard not so long before: "When you come to the aid of another Jew, *Hashem* will come to your aid."

And so He had!

פָּרָשַׁת מִשְׁפָּטִים

Parashas Mishpatim

Twice Four Hundred

אֲשֶׁר תָּשִׂים לִפְנֵיהֶם

"Which you shall place before them" (21:1)

Like a set table which is ready for the meal.
(Rashi)

R' Prida had a disciple who was so slow at learning that his teacher was required to review each point four hundred times.

One time R' Prida was called on to take care of an urgent matter of communal importance. He did not postpone his usual lesson that morning but intended to go when he had finished. To his dismay, his student was not able to grasp the point that day even after a repetition of four hundred times.

"What is the matter with you today?" R' Prida asked kindly. "Why can't you understand? We reviewed it four hundred times, just like every day."

The student replied apologetically, "I know, Rebbe, but I could not help thinking that you would have to go away later and so I was unable to keep my mind on the lesson. I could not absorb it because I was tense and afraid."

R' Prida decided to remain with his student and review the material again until he finally understood it thoroughly. He sat by his side and explained it, as if he were beginning anew. It took him an additional four hundred times until the student thoroughly grasped the lesson.

R' Prida's infinite patience and devotion made a deep impression in heaven. A heavenly voice called out: "What would you like for a reward, R' Prida, to live for an additional four hundred years or to take your entire generation along with you into Gan Eden?"

R' Prida replied that he chose the latter.

It was the wiser choice for heaven ruled, "If so, he is to be rewarded with both!"

(According to Tractate *Eruvin 54b*)

An Eye for an Eye

עַיִן תַּחַת עַיִן

An eye for an eye (21:24)

There was once a wealthy and distinguished man in the time of Rav Shrira Gaon who owned a most precious *sefer Torah,* one which was reputed to have been written by Ezra the Scribe. This heirloom was priceless and he cherished it accordingly.

The man had two sons who, in their father's lifetime, lived in peace, love and harmony. But when the rich man passed away, a raging argument broke out between them as to who would inherit the priceless Torah scroll. Each one coveted his father's most precious possession. Since there was no way of dividing it between them, they decided to go before a rabbinical court.

They came before Rav Shrira Gaon. He listened carefully to their tale but could find no way to arrive at a compromise and please both sides. The only solution, therefore, was to settle the matter by lottery.

The brothers accepted this ruling and held the lottery in Rav Shrira's presence. One brother was awarded the *sefer Torah* while the other inherited everything else that the father had left behind.

The brother who had won the Torah scroll was the happier of the two. The other, who was now a wealthy man, was heartbroken. He had wanted that unique possession far more than wealth!

A convert, who lived in that city, was irked by the great fuss made over a 'simple' scroll. How could one be willing to set aside a huge fortune in favor of just one item? The entire controversy, which had been the talk of the town for weeks, annoyed him so much that he decided to vent his anger in some form. He would damage that precious scroll and render it valueless. This would serve the brothers right for making such a silly fuss over a roll of parchment!

The convert disguised himself as a Jewish traveler and went to the synagogue which held the celebrated *sefer Torah*. He hid behind the stove until night. When the last of the worshippers had left he came out of hiding and went directly to the *aron kodesh*, removed the scroll from its magnificent velvet and wood case and opened it. It unrolled right at the spot that read, "And you shall worship, *va'avadtem* other gods." He erased the letter *ayin* and replaced it with an *alef*, thus rendering the entire scroll worthless, *pasul*!

The Torah was to be read that next day. During *shacharis,* when the reader reached the passage, he discovered the mistake. There was one wrong letter!

The owner of the scroll heard of this and felt as if an arrow had pierced his heart. He took the news so badly that he became ill. He knew that such a mistake could be repaired by an expert *sofer* but was pained by the thought that his priceless Torah had been a fake. It could not possibly have been written by Ezra the Scribe. He certainly could not have made an error. Therefore, it could only be that Ezra had not written the scroll!

The incident affected him more and more as time went by. He became critically ill and there was no cure for his malady of the heart.

Then he had a dream. His deceased father appeared to him one night saying, "Do not be so distressed, my beloved son. Rest assured that the scroll that you inherited from me was truly written by Ezra HaSofer and was once perfect. A wicked convert made the scroll unfit, *pasul.* He begrudged you such a wonderful treasure and wished, by one stroke, to render it useless."

The following night he dreamt the same dream. This time, however, his father gave him a sign: "Go to the synagogue tomorrow morning and look under the reader's table. There you will find a human eye. Know that this is the accursed convert's right eye which fell out at the moment that he erased the *ayin* (which also means 'eye') in the Torah. He was thus punished measure for measure, or as the Torah says literally, *'ayin tachas ayin* — an eye for an eye.' As for the mistake in the scroll, this must never be corrected. The heavenly court has ruled that no one is qualified to repair the scroll which the holy Ezra HaSofer wrote."

When he awoke the next morning he went to the synagogue. He looked under the reader's table and sure enough, there was the human eye. The dream had been true, after all!

The Most Kosher of Matzos

אַלְמָנָה וְיָתוֹם לֹא תְעַנּוּן

You shall not oppress a widow or an orphan (22:21)

R' Yisrael Salant, the founder of the *Musar* movement, was scrupulously careful in every *mitzvah* that he performed. When he baked *matzos* for *Pesach* he took all the pains and precautions possible to make sure that there was no question of *chametz*!

One year, however, he was unable to be present at the *matzah* baking and delegated this important task to his choice disciples who had been at the baking with him for many years, and knew what to look for. Yet, because they were afraid of not doing things which would be up to the high standards to which R' Yisrael was accustomed, they went to their Rebbe and asked him for last minute instructions.

R' Yisrael looked at them gravely and said, "There is one particular thing that I do want you to keep in mind." The *talmidim* expected to hear about new *kavanos* to bear in mind to consecrate the *matzos* even more. They were, therefore, surprised when he said, "There is a widow who works in the bakery; she kneads the dough. Be careful not to rush her, even though time is of the essence. Make sure that you treat her kindly and considerately so as not to transgress the commandment of 'You shall not oppress a widow'.

You see," he added, "when you follow precautions with regard to the laws of *Pesach,* you must not forget the other commandments."

Two Hours Less

אַלְמָנָה וְיָתוֹם לֹא תְעַנּוּן

You shall not oppress a widow or an orphan (22:21)

One of R' Yisrael Salanter's disciples, who lived in a distant city, learned that his Rebbe would be passing through on a trip and might be persuaded to remain in his house over *Shabbos.* Knowing how careful R' Yisrael was in everything he did, he first described his own special practices in *kashrus* and *mitzvah*-observance. He bought his meat at a certain butcher known for impeccable standards of *kashrus* and *yiras shamayim,* piety. The cook in his home was the widow of a deceased Torah scholar of note who took meticulous care in checking every single item that went into the pot. As for the *Shabbos* meals themselves — he boasted, — they were the height of sanctity. Torah thoughts were expressed between courses, *zemiros* were sung with great fervor.

The entire table glowed with an atmosphere of *kedushah*! It was no wonder," the disciple noted, somewhat proudly, "that the Friday night meal stretched out until past midnight!

If he thought to impress his Rebbe, he was somewhat mistaken. For while R' Yisrael did accept his cordial invitation, he made one condition: that his host shorten the meal by two hours.

Somewhat puzzled, the young man agreed, thrilled that R' Yisrael would be his honored guest, despite this strange limitation. It would restrict him, but so what — the main thing was that R' Yisrael had agreed to come. The lucky day arrived and R' Yisrael came to spend the *Shabbos* in the young man's house. That Friday evening the host rushed through the meal without even pausing between courses. As soon as the food had been eaten the *mayim acharonim* was brought before *bircas hamazon*. The host, with a hint of tears in his eyes, turned to his illustrious guest. He could not contain his feelings and had to ask: "Tell me please, Rebbe, what fault or shortcoming did you find with me or my *Shabbos* table to force us to rush through the meal and shorten it by two hours?"

Instead of replying, R' Yisrael asked permission to speak to the cook. When she entered the room, he turned to her and said, "Please forgive me for having put you to so much trouble this evening. Because of me you were forced to speed up the serving and bring one course right after the next. I hope you are not angry."

To the surprise of all those gathered around the table, the cook confessed, "On the contrary, may you be blessed, honored rabbi. If only you could come every week! You see the usual *Shabbos* meal drags on and on until late at night and I, who am exhausted from the busy day's work, can hardly stand on my feet. Tonight, though, I will be able to go home early and go to sleep. What a pleasure!"

When she had finished, R' Yisrael turned to his host with a slight nod and said, "Her words are the answer to your question. Your *Shabbos* table, with its fine Torah thoughts and lovely songs do you credit, I am sure. But, when they are at the expense of a tired widow, they are not as praiseworthy as you might think!"

Flour for Safekeeping

כָּל אַלְמָנָה וְיָתוֹם לֹא תְעַנּוּן

You shall not oppress a widow or an orphan (22:21)

When R' Yehoshua Leib Diskin settled in Jerusalem, he availed himself of the devoted service of his faithful disciple, R' Eliezer Dan Ralbag. Among other duties, R' Yehoshua Leib entrusted R' Eliezer Dan with the safekeeping of the special flour harvested early for *matzah* baking, lest it come into any contact with water.

When R' Eliezer Dan passed away, the Maharil Diskin wished to transfer the flour to the home of another disciple, the saintly R' Tzvi Michel. He sent him to R' Eliezer Dan's widow to fetch the flour. R' Tzvi Michel did not jump up to do his Rebbe's bidding as he always did. Standing there, his head somewhat bowed, he said,

"Rebbe, don't you think that perhaps the widow will take offense if the *shmurah* flour is taken away from her in the middle of the year? Won't she be insulted and fear that now that her husband is dead she is considered less worthy? Would this not fall into the category of 'You shall not oppress a widow or an orphan'?"

R' Yehoshua Leib nodded in agreement. "You are perfectly right." Reb Tzvi Michel did not perform this errand and the flour remained in the widow's home until it was time to bake that year's *matzos.*

Without the Dowry

לא תִהְיֶה לוֹ כְּנֹשֶׁה

You shall not be unto him like a usurer (22:24)

When a young girl got married in Europe, her parents gave her a dowry, each family according to their means. Since the young couple did not always need the money right away, it was often brought to a trusted, wealthy member of the congregation for safekeeping, to be dispensed according to need.

When R' Yaakov Berlin's daughter got married, her father entrusted her large dowry to a prominent Jew from Slutzk, a man of excellent character and reputation.

Time passed. One day the rumor began circulating that the Jew from Slutzk had fallen on hard times. He had lost all his money and was on the verge of bankruptcy. R' Yaakov of Mir was afraid for his daughter's dowry.

The family sat in council, wondering what to do. In the end it was decided that R' Yaakov travel to Slutzk himself to see about his daughter's dowry.

R' Yaakov set out. He returned a week later and was welcomed by his family. All were curious to learn what had happened. R' Yaakov sat them all down and told his tale:

"As soon as I reached Slutzk I made many inquiries about what exactly was the extent of our trustee's failure. I learned that the rumors had been correct; he had lost everything. I did not have the heart to go to him and demand my money, for the Torah enjoins us, 'Do not be like a usurer', that is, a demanding lender. I decided to forget all about the money and did not even go to speak to him. I trust that you will understand why I have returned without the dowry, without even seeing him."

Two Partners, Two Patients

לֹא תִהְיֶה לוֹ כְּנֹשֶׁה

You shall not be unto him like a usurer (22:24)

When R' Tzvi Ashkenazi of Altona, better known by the name of his work, "*Chacham Tzvi*", got married he received a considerable dowry from his wife's father. His family counseled him to invest it and let it grow for him. R' Tzvi was advised to put his capital into a silent partnership with a known and trusted businessman who would do all the work but pay R' Tzvi a percent on his investment.

"You can live off the income," his family said. "This will enable you to remain independent and continue your Torah study indefinitely!"

The idea appealed to the promising young scholar and a partnership agreement was drawn up and signed. The father of the businessman himself also signed as guarantor for the sum which the *Chacham Tzvi* had invested.

It turned out, though, that the businessman was dishonest and evil. He took the money and fled Altona for Amsterdam where he squandered the entire sum on amusement and gambling. R' Tzvi was left penniless.

The money upon which he had been relying for his daily expenses was now gone and he had no savings to fall back on. He had always refused to accept any help from others even though, as a Torah scholar, he had often been offered money for support. He was hard struck by the blow.

He took the matter so much to heart that he became ill. The doctors who tried to cure him saw that they were helpless and, at one point, even despaired of his life. As a last resort, they prescribed a visit to a health spa. This worked and soon R' Tzvi was on his way to recovery.

At this time R' Tzvi learned that someone else had also become ill because of the scandal. It was the father of the scoundrel, the man who had signed as guarantor for the huge sum the *Chacham Tzvi* had invested with his son. Now he lay critically ill as a result of his anxiety. As soon as R' Tzvi heard this, he understood the cause of the illness.

"What can I do to help this poor man?" he wondered. "How can I save him from worrying himself to death?"

He finally hit upon a solution. He took the document with the father's signature and ripped it up. He then sent the pieces to the ailing father, explaining, "I have canceled your guarantee for my money. Forget the entire thing and don't worry any more!"

When the sick man saw the torn document, he breathed a sigh of relief and started along the upward road to recovery. Soon he was entirely well.

(*Megilas Sefer* from his son, the *Yaavetz*)

What Did the News Mean?

לֹא תִשָּׂא שֵׁמַע שָׁוְא
You shall not utter a false report (23:1)

Before becoming a rebbe, R' Zusha was a hidden saint, a Jew who wandered from place to place without anyone realizing his inner greatness.

One time, when R' Zusha was sitting in a *beis medrash* in a strange town, a woman burst in. She was frantic. "Has anyone seen my husband? Does anyone know where he is?"

By asking a few questions, the people learned that the

woman's husband had disappeared a long time ago, deserting his wife without a penny to her name. Nor was she able to remarry because her husband had never given her a divorce. In her plight, the woman had begun to search for him, going from town to town, hoping that some day she would find him. Wherever she went, she asked the people if they had seen her husband, describing him by certain distinguishing signs.

When R' Zusha heard the poor woman's question, he got up from his place and said to her, "Go directly to the town hostel. You will find him there."

Without even questioning how the stranger knew, she left the *beis medrash* and headed straight for the local *hachnasas orchim* home. And there he was! Her long lost husband!

The entire city was overcome. How had this inconsequential stranger, a simple man, known where to find this woman's husband, if he had not even set foot into the hostel? Was he some miracle-worker, a saint that they did not know about? It was the talk of the town.

When the people rushed to R' Zusha for an explanation, he said humbly, "You are mistaken if you think there was a miracle or divine intuition on my part. This is what happened. I heard two men talking together this morning. One of them mentioned, in passing, that a stranger had just arrived at the town hostel. I wondered what relevance this conversation had to me, why heaven chose me to overhear it. Surely, there must be a reason. I was still puzzled about that piece of unnecessary information when in burst that woman, looking for her husband. I jumped to the conclusion that he must be the newcomer who had just arrived at the hostel and sent her there."

In attempting to hush up the seeming miracle and conceal his divine vision, R' Zusha had forgotten one thing. He was not like other people. He heard only what was necessary for him to hear. And so while people did not consider this an outright miracle, they came away with a newfound respect for R' Zusha, who only heard what he needed to hear.

The Restored Friendship

כִּי תִרְאֶה חֲמוֹר שֹׂנַאֲךָ רֹבֵץ תַּחַת מַשָּׂאוֹ... עָזֹב תַּעֲזֹב עִמּוֹ

If you see the donkey of your enemy crouching under his burden... indeed shall you help him (23:5)

R' Alexander, a sage who lived many years ago, told the following story:

There once lived two donkey-drivers, men who earned their livelihood by delivering goods upon their donkeys. Reuven and Shimon were devoted friends from childhood on and even though they both went into the same business, each used to help the other and send him customers if he himself was not available.

But as often happens, the two friends quarreled and began to hate one another. In time they forgot the cause of their enmity but the hatred remained. They refused to greet one another and, if one saw the other coming down the street, he would avoid him by crossing over to the other side.

One morning Reuven went to work. He had two large sacks of grain which he had to transport to a different city. The sacks were poorly balanced and the day was very hot. The poor donkey was very uncomfortable because the sacks had not been properly tied onto his back and they jostled him with each move. He walked more slowly and more slowly until he finally came to a stop and fell down under the heavy sacks. He was unable to rise.

Reuven tried his best to coax the donkey up but failed. The animal could not and would not budge. He fumbled with the ropes, trying to untie the sacks but these had gotten tangled. Poor Reuven was at a loss. There was nothing that he could do. Reuven stood helplessly by the fallen donkey; the summer sun beat down upon his head; the sweat poured down his face and back. He looked up and down the road. Perhaps there was someone who could help him, but the road was deserted.

He stood there for a long time, not knowing what to do. Suddenly he noted a spot on the horizon. The spot was moving quickly. It was a man leading a donkey. Surely he would lend a helping hand. Reuven squinted for a few minutes and then, his heart fell. It was Shimon, his enemy.

Shimon walked along the road, keeping pace with the bundle-laden donkey. He reached Reuven.

Reuven hoped that his one-time friend would have pity on him and his donkey. Who better than he, a fellow donkey-owner, would know how helpless he was? But Shimon continued on his way.

Reuven's heart fell. How long would he have to wait for the next person to come along? And then it happened. Shimon stopped his donkey. He seemed to be thinking. Shimon remembered what it said in the Torah: "If you see the donkey of your enemy crouching under his burden — shall you refrain from helping him?! Indeed you shall help him!" Shimon could not help thinking that the verse applied perfectly to this very situation. Reuven watched, hoping against hope...

Shimon turned and went back to where Reuven was standing. Without uttering a word, he began working at the knots in the rope. His nimble fingers soon untied them. The donkey was able to get back up on his feet. Now came the difficult part — loading the bags on again. One man had to sling the heavy sacks up while the other caught the ropes and secured them tightly. Both men had to work together. They also had to talk to each other. "Heave!" said one. "Grab the rope!" said the other. "Lower it a bit!" "Balance that carefully!" and so on.

They finally finished. Shimon stood back and congratulated himself, "That was a job well done!"

"Indeed it was! How can I ever thank you? Without your help I would have been lost. How long can one stand in this burning sun? I am truly grateful."

Suddenly, the two men realized that not only were they talking to one another, they were even smiling like old friends! The barriers had fallen down.

Reuven thought to himself, "How could I have ever thought ill of such a fine fellow? Look how hard he worked for my sake! How kind he was to stop, not expecting any thanks from me!" And aloud he said, "I see you are walking in the same direction as I. Let's stop at the first inn. I must treat you to a well-deserved drink. It is the very least I can do to repay you."

Shimon agreed. Later when the two were eating and drinking together, they erased the last bit of ill feeling between them. And from then on, they were the best of friends, just as in the old days.

(Adapted from *Midrash Tanchuma, Parashas Mishpatim*)

Why the Sons Died

מִדְּבַר שֶׁקֶר תִּרְחָק
Keep far away from falsehood (23:7)

In the city of Kushta, which means truth, people spoke only truth. They never lied or told half truths either. *Hashem* wished to reward them and so He kept them alive as a shining example. No one in Kushta ever died. If an old person felt he had been on this earth long enough, he would leave the city to die.

Rav Tavyomi married a woman from Kushta and went to live near his wife's family. In time his wife bore him two sons.

One day, his wife was washing her hair, when a neighbor knocked at the door, asking for her. Rav Tavyomi did not know what to say. Should he let the woman in? That was immodest. Should he tell the neighbor that she had come at the wrong time? She might get insulted. He said that his wife was out.

A short while later both of Rav Tavyomi's sons died. The father realized, at once, that this tragedy had occurred because he had lied. The people of Kushta were horrified by the disaster. Nothing of the kind had ever happened. Even old people did not die in this city! When they came to investigate the matter, he was forced to tell them the truth.

They said to him at once, "Leave this city immediately, lest such an occurrence happen again!"

(Adapted from *Sanhedrin 97a*)

A Basket of Fruit

וְשֹׁחַד לֹא תִקָּח
You shall not accept bribery (23:8)

R' Yishmael bar Yosi owned a field, an orchard and a vineyard. Since he devoted his time to learning Torah, he rented this land out to a sharecropper who gave him part of the produce in return. Each *erev Shabbos* the tenant farmer would bring R' Yishmael a basket of luscious fruit as part of his payment.

One week the farmer came a day earlier; he brought his basket on a Thursday. R' Yishmael was surprised and asked him why he had come that day.

The man replied, "I had to be in town today, anyway, and thought I would save myself a trip. You see, today I have a hearing in court."

If the farmer was to be in court, that meant that he, R' Yishmael, would have to sit and judge him. He looked at the farmer and said, "I cannot sit on your case, nor will I accept the fruit that you brought today!"

R' Yishmael then asked other judges to preside in the *beis din* that day. All that afternoon R' Yishmael sat outside the *beis din*. He could not help hearing the loud voices emerging from the court, and he recognized the voice of his tenant farmer. Each time he heard him argue, he thought to himself, "Why does he not say this or that? Thus he could win his case."

R' Yishmael was surprised at himself. He had always

been an impartial judge, never leaning towards one side or another. What had made him change so? And then he suddenly realized what had happened. The weekly basket of fruit had made him favor his tenant.

He used this example when he explained the matter of bribery to his students some time later. "The fruits which the tenant brought me were my own. And yet I found myself siding with him and justifying him, despite myself. This goes to show how far-reaching an influence bribery can have. How much worse is it when real bribery is involved. Even if the judge wants to judge fairly and honestly, he is unable to do so, once he has accepted bribery in any form. How wonderful are the words of the Torah, 'For bribery blinds the eyes of the wise.' Once they have taken a bribe, judges can no longer see what is true and what is false, what is unjust and what is just."

(According to Tractate *Kesubos 105b*)

This, Too, is Bribery

וְשֹׁחַד לֹא תִקָּח

You shall not accept bribery (23:8)

The man entered the court with an air of belonging there. He walked over to the judge, Rav, and greeted him as if he were an old friend. "*Shalom aleichem!* Don't you remember me? Don't you recall that you were once a guest of mine? How I tried to make you comfortable and at home. I remember how honored I was by your visit."

Rav nodded, "Yes, I do recall that time. And I am truly

grateful for your kind hospitality. What has brought you here today? Can I be of any service to you?"

"Indeed you can," said the man smiling broadly. "I have a *din Torah* here today, really a small matter. I was hoping that you might be the judge." He was hinting that he expected the rabbi to bend the law in his favor.

But Rav replied, "I am not allowed to judge your case. Since you were once my host, I would not be impartial."

He called Rav Kahana over and asked him to preside over the case. The man took offense, feeling that he deserved privileged treatment and when he stood before Rav Kahana, he spoke disrespectfully to him and answered his questions in an arrogant tone. There were some questions that he even refused to answer. Finally he said, "I insist that Rav be the judge in my case." But Rav Kahana replied severely, "Rav is unable to help you. If you answer my questions correctly and respectfully, then all is well. But if you do not, you will be ignored and ostracized by everyone. That is the punishment of a man who is disrespectful in court!"

(Adapted from Tractate *Sanhedrin 7b*)

A Gold Coin in a Snuff Box

וְשֹׁחַד לֹא תִקָּח
You shall not accept bribery (23:8)

Two men once came to be tried before R' Avraham Yehoshua Heshel, the Apter Rebbe. It took hours for each of them to fully describe his side of the case. When they had had their say, the Rebbe asked them to wait in the reception room, while he reviewed all the *halachic* aspects of the case.

The rabbi was closeted in his room for a long time; the books of reference were piled up high on his desk. From time to time he would ask his *shammash* to hand him another book from the bookcase. To help his thinking, the Rebbe would take an occasional pinch of snuff and inhale deeply. This seemed to clear his mind. Once more, he stretched his hand out to the snuffbox only to find that the snuff was all gone. He drew the *shammash*'s attention to the fact, gave him a coin and nodded towards the door, hinting that he wanted him to buy some more snuff. The *shammash* left the room. In the waiting room sat one of the two men. The other had gone out to eat. The man fidgeted restlessly. As soon as he saw the *shammash* he jumped up nervously. He watched as the *shammash* went over to the window and looked outside. What a miserable day. It was cold, snowy, and so slippery. With a sigh, the *shammash* took his fur overcoat off its hook and tiredly put in on. Then he went to the door. But before he could open it, the man was there.

"Let me run the errand for you," he begged. "I am much younger than you. Besides I have nothing to do. This waiting is getting on my nerves. I would welcome a refreshing walk outside."

Reluctantly, the *shammash* gave him the empty snuffbox and the coin and told him what kind of snuff the Rebbe used. He went out and was back in much less time than it would have taken the elderly man.

The *shammash* took the snuffbox in to the Rebbe, who nodded in appreciation. Without even looking, he stretched his hand out to take some of the fresh snuff.

The *shammash* went outside to sit down and wait.

Suddenly, he remembered what the Rebbe had told him many, many years before: Never accept any service, no matter how small, from any of the litigants before their case had been decided. Throughout the years he had been careful. What had happened to him? He resolved that he would never let it happen again. But what was done, was done.

Meanwhile, the Rebbe was still struggling with the problem. It seemed as if it had suddenly grown more complex. He took a deep breath, inhaling some snuff, expecting his mind to clear as it always did. But the matter seemed more difficult. He took another pinch — and his fingers closed around something metallic and cold. What was this? Drawing the box to him he discovered a gold coin at the bottom. How had it gotten there? Calling his *shammash* to him, he asked, "Where did you get this snuff?"

The elderly man was alarmed. How had the Rebbe discovered his lapse so quickly? Never before had he disobeyed him. How had the Rebbe suspected him of doing wrong, just this time?

In a trembling voice he told the Rebbe that he had let the litigant fetch the tobacco, since he had been so insistent. He confessed that at that moment, he had forgotten the rule which the Rebbe had laid down many years before. With tears in his eyes, he promised never to fail him again.

"Call in the litigant," said the Apter Rebbe.

The man entered. The Rebbe handed him the coin and said bitterly, "I can no longer judge your case. By this gold coin, you have disqualified me. Take your business to a different court. And be sure to keep the coin to yourself."

Open the Eyes of the Blind

כִּי הַשֹּׁחַד יְעַוֵּר
For bribery blinds (23:8)

In his old age, R' Chaim Kapusi's eyesight began to fail him until he became totally blind.

When this became known, some evil men began talking behind the rabbi's back. They accused him of having taken bribes when he served as judge; for the Torah says that bribery blinds the wise. "That is why he walks in darkness today," they said.

R' Chaim did not take these insults without defending his good name. He replied in the words of King David, "Even though I walk in the Valley of Darkness I shall fear no evil..." As to their reference about sitting in darkness, he quoted, "Even when I sit in darkness, *Hashem* is my light."

His apt replies were not enough to silence wagging tongues. People continued to slander him, asking: Why else would he turn blind in his old age?

When R' Chaim saw that he must put an end to the malicious gossip, he called a meeting. One *Shabbos* he summoned the entire congregation to the synagogue. He began pleasantly. When he reached the end of his sermon he said, "I know, my honored audience, that people are ruining my good reputation. *Hashem* is my witness that I am innocent of the sin of which they accuse me. My blindness is not a punishment for having accepted bribes. If there is amongst you anyone who ever gave me a bribe, or in whose favor I bent the law, let him step forward before me and before *Hashem* and before this honored gathering. May you all be my witnesses: I beseech *Hashem,* the G-d of Justice, that if the insinuations against me are true, let my bones dry up so that I fall down right before you. However, if I am innocent, let it be the divine will that my eyes be opened once more, so that I can again behold the sun. And may this entire congregation see that there is a Judge of Truth and of Justice!"

The moment that R' Chaim finished his words, a miracle happened. He was suddenly able to see again! He looked around him with awe and wonder, singling out members of the congregation, addressing them by name and title.

Everyone saw the miracle and understood how great their saintly and honest rabbi was.

From that time on R' Chaim had the words *Baal haNes* attached to his name. And from then on he used to sign his name, *Hashem Nissi Chaim Kapusi.*

R' Chaim Yosef David Azulai, the Chida, in his work *Shem Hagedolim,* writes as follows: "I saw a signature which he had made when blind; the letters were hardly legible. I saw a better signature of his made after the miracle — *Hashem Nissi Chaim Kapusi;* it was firm and clear!"

Up In Smoke

הִנֵּה אָנֹכִי שׁוֹלֵחַ מַלְאָךְ לְפָנֶיךָ לִשְׁמָרְךָ
Behold, I am sending an angel before you to guard you (23:20)

Czar Nikolai of Russia hated the Jews. He prided himself on being a rabid anti-Semite and used all of his ingenuity to oppress his Jewish subjects with harsh decrees and impossible laws. Time and again, though, he was thwarted. Jews found out his plans in advance and were always able to counteract them through their vast influence in many areas.

This infuriated the Czar and prodded him to seek new ways to harass and destroy the Jews. With all his heart, he yearned to see them disappear off the face of the earth.

Finally, he felt that he had the solution, a foolproof method of ridding his country of Jews. The Czar quickly summoned his top ministers to an emergency council. They came at once and found their monarch excited and nervous. He looked at each one in turn and then began to speak:

"I have invited you here today to inform you that I have found an answer to a problem that has been bothering all of us. You probably know that I am referring to the Jewish problem. We must get rid of this race once and for all, or else, force them to convert. As you can realize, this plan must remain top secret. No one must know any hint of this, lest our plan be ruined before it can be carried out. As much as we would like them to convert, we cannot rely on that, for Jews are terribly stubborn. Their religion is what unites them and keeps them alive. The first thrust of our attack must be at their children. We must hit at their education, closing their *chadorim* and *yeshivos*. We must shut their places of gathering, their synagogues. And finally, we must forbid them to fulfill two commandments in particular: *Shabbos* and circumcision.

"You have been invited here today to hear the general outline of my plan. It is up to you, my worthy ministers, to draw up a working design to execute it. But until you do so, until that program is ready, down to the last detail to be put into action, you must keep it secret. For, if the Jews get any hint of this, they will overturn the very world to prevent the enactment of such a law."

The ministers nodded in wholehearted agreement. The Czar continued, "These laws are to go into effect in another five months. The exact date falls on the first day of their Passover festival.

It is your job to work out the details of this and to send a copy of the decree in a sealed envelope to every town and village in all of Russia. These are to bear the words: 'To be opened on such and such a date for immediate action.' This way the Jews, whose spies infiltrate every branch of the government, will have no way of learning about the law.

Just to make sure, you will remain here in the palace until you have completed the task. You are now completely isolated from the outside world. No one has access to you nor can you leave the premises. You have been put under heavy guard while you prepare the detailed outline. I expect you to have completed this project in every detail by midnight."

Shocked, the ministers looked at one another. This was without precedent. They were accustomed to their king's wild ideas but this was different from anything that he had previously demanded.

Unable to protest, the ministers sat down and got to work on a plan which would sweep all of Russia off its feet.

After a few hours of concentrated work, long before the Czar's deadline, the final plan was drawn up and ready for enactment. The final copy was placed on the desk of the Interior Minister. Suddenly, the door opened and in strode the Czar himself. Without uttering a word, he strode purposefully right up to the Interior Minister's desk, skimmed through the contents of the program, spat out a curse word and flung the pages into the blazing hearth. Then, turning on his heel, he left the room.

The ministers looked at one another in alarm. What was the meaning of this sudden outburst? They had put so much time and effort into that finished product which the Czar had tossed into the fire without a word of explanation. What now?

The ministers were now divided. Some were for going home; others, who feared the Czar's wrath, suggested that they remain until the midnight deadline. Finally, one of them reminded the rest that refreshments had been prepared in the adjoining room. It seemed most sensible to retire there and relax with good food and drink. The suggestion appealed to them all.

They gathered around the table and began eating. Suddenly, they heard heavy footsteps. Czar Nikolai entered the room accompanied by two bodyguards. He looked at them with satisfaction and said, "After such hard work you certainly deserve to relax. Just please give me the completed program which you have prepared for me."

What was the Czar referring to? Was he waiting for another program? Surely he had not expected them to formulate another one so soon, especially since he had not told them why he had been displeased with the first one. One minister summoned his courage and said, "How could Your Majesty have expected us to formulate a program in such a short amount of time?!"

The Czar grew livid with rage. Clenching his raised fists, he shouted, "What do you mean? You promised to finish the job by midnight! Was that not time enough for all you clever men? What right do you have to sit here, gobbling food like pigs, if you did not do your work?"

"But, when Your Majesty threw our plan into the fireplace, we thought that you had abandoned the project," he replied.

"*I* burned your work?! What nonsense are you saying?" the Czar thundered at them. "What is this, treason? A plot against me?" He quickly turned to his bodyguards and gave orders to arrest the entire roomful of ministers. Within seconds six husky Cossacks stormed into the room, waiting for further instructions. One of the two bodyguards whispered into the Czar's ear, "They just said that Your Majesty was here a few hours ago. That is an outright lie for you did not leave your office all that time. Why don't you verify it with the Cossack guards? Ask them if they saw you."

The Czar turned to the burly soldiers and asked them, "Have you admitted anyone into this chamber since you were put here to guard the ministers?"

"Aside from Your Majesty, no one, Sire."

"What do you mean by that?" the Czar asked. "I was not here before."

"But Your Majesty came here about two hours ago!" the Cossack guards insisted. "We are certain. We all saw you."

It was now the Czar's turn to become pale. "But I was sitting in my chamber all this time, from the afternoon on. I never left it at all. What can this mystery mean?"

He thought for a moment, then said with a sigh, "I know. It must have been an angel sent by the Jewish G-d to protect His chosen people by burning the decree against them. I see that Heaven does not want the Jews destroyed and no matter how I plot and plan, He will always protect them."

The Danger Without Torah

אִם לֹא בְרִיתִי יוֹמָם וָלָיְלָה חֻקּוֹת שָׁמַיִם וָאָרֶץ לֹא שָׂמְתִּי

If My covenant be not day and night, if I have not appointed the laws of heaven and earth...

(Haftorah Parashas Mishpatim, Yirmiyah 33)

Our Sages explained this as referring to the covenant of the Torah, to teach us that the heavens and earth were created because of the Torah.

(Rashi)

When the Roman empire forbade Jews to study Torah, R' Akiva flaunted the law and gathered huge public assemblies to teach Torah.

When Pappus ben Yehudah saw this, he asked R' Akiva, "Are you not afraid of the consequences? That the Romans will punish you?"

R' Akiva answered, "I am surprised that you, Pappus, who are reputed to be a wise man ask such a question. You would seem to be a fool!"

Pappus did not understand why R' Akiva thought him a fool. And so, R' Akiva continued.

"Let me tell you a parable," said R' Akiva:

A fox was once strolling along a river bank when he noticed the fish fluttering about in the water. "What are you fleeing? Of what are you afraid?" he asked. The fish replied, "We are afraid of the fishermen's nets which are spread in the water to catch us." The fox then suggested, "I have an idea. Why don't you come up on land and we can live together?" They laughed at the foolish notion and said, "If we are in danger in the water, which is the very source of our sustenance and life, how much more so would we be threatened up on land, where we are sure to die!"

"The moral must be apparent to you, Pappus," said R' Akiva. "If we Jews are risking our lives when we study Torah, how much more certain would the danger be, if we ceased studying Torah which is our very life, like water for fish!"

Shortly afterwards the Romans caught R' Akiva and threw him into jail. He was sentenced to death.

He was taken out to be executed; it was the hour for *kriyas shema.* The Romans tortured R' Akiva; they tore his flesh with combs of iron but this did not distract him from saying the *shema,* the prayer in which a Jew declares his loyalty and allegiance to *Hashem.*

His disciples, who were looking on, cried out, "Rebbe?

Are you then able to concentrate upon declaring your love for *Hashem* even when you are being torn by iron combs?!"

R' Akiva replied, "All my life I have waited and yearned for the opportunity to be able to fulfill the words of the *shema* — to love *Hashem* 'with all your soul' which means, even when He is taking away your soul. I have always wanted to carry out that commandment. And now that that opportunity arises, shall I not do so?!"

When he came to the word *'echad'* of the prayer, he prolonged that word until his soul departed.

As soon as his soul had left R' Akiva's body, a heavenly voice announced, "Fortunate are you, R' Akiva, for having died upon the word *'echad'*... Fortunate are you, R' Akiva, for you are guaranteed eternal life!"

(According to Tractate *Berachos 61b*)

פָּרָשַׁת תְּרוּמָה

Parashas Terumah

A Time to be Generous

מֵאֵת כָּל אִישׁ אֲשֶׁר יִדְּבֶנּוּ לִבּוֹ תִּקְחוּ

From each man whose heart is willing shall you take (25:2)

R' Akiva and another Sage once traveled to collect money for poor Torah scholars. They went from place to place, visiting each house to ask for a donation.

In the course of their travels they came to the outskirts of a city. From afar they could already see the home of a certain wealthy Jew called Barbuchin. They approached and were about to knock when they could not help overhearing something that made them stop and listen. Barbuchin was talking to his young son.

"Father," said the lad. "What shall I buy for dinner today at the market?"

Barbuchin instructed his son, "Buy some vegetables."

"What kind shall I buy, father? The kind that are one for a *moneh*-coin or two for a *moneh*?"

"Buy some of the dry vegetables, they are cheaper — two for a *moneh*."

The two Sages looked at one another. One of them whispered, "We had better not knock at this door. If the owner does not want to buy fresh vegetables, he must be a very stingy person!"

"Let us first visit the other houses in this city," said the other. "Then, if we have time on our way back, we can stop by here too."

With these words they left Barbuchin's threshold and turned towards the main street. They knocked at each door and received as much money as the householder felt he could afford.

They were about to leave the city when the road took them past Barbuchin's house again. The master of the house was in the front yard, busy at work. They greeted him in passing, "*Shalom aleichem*! Could you help us out with a donation for needy Torah scholars?"

They did not expect more than a few pennies from such a stingy man. How great was their surprise when he replied, "I am busy but, if you go inside, my wife will give you a bowl full of golden *dinarim*."

R' Akiva and his companion walked into the house and approached the housewife, saying, "Your husband said to give us a bowl full of golden *dinarim* for charity."

She was not at all surprised and merely asked, "Did he say whether I was to give a full, heaping, bowl or not?"

"He did not say. We really don't know what he meant."

"In that case, I will give you a heaping one. If that was not his intention, then I will make up the difference from my personal funds." So saying, she took a large bowl and heaped it up full of golden *dinarim*.

When the Sages went out the front door, Barbuchin asked them, "Did my wife give you, a full heaping bowl?

They replied, "She did not know exactly how much you really wanted to donate and so, gave us the heaping measure, saying that if you objected, she would make up the difference herself."

A satisfied smile spread over Barbuchin's face. "She is a good, clever woman. As a matter of fact, I really wanted her to give the heaping measure!"

He was silent for a moment. Finally he asked, "There is one thing I would like you to explain to me. Upon entering the city, you had to pass my house. Why did you not come in at once, but first made the rounds of all the other houses?"

R' Akiva explained, "We did stop by here first, but we could not help overhearing your son ask which vegetables to buy for dinner. Hearing your reply, we thought that if you spent so little for yourself, you would give even less for charity! It would not even be worth our while to knock at your door!"

A broader smile spread over Barbuchin's face. He explained, "It is my privilege to spend or to stint on my personal expenditures. We will come to no harm by eating cheaper vegetables. But when it comes to fulfilling *Hashem*'s commandments — I have no right to be stingy!"

(According to *Midrash Esther Rabbah* 2:3)

Half the Field to Charity

מֵאֵת כָּל אִישׁ אֲשֶׁר יִדְּבֶנּוּ לִבּוֹ תִּקְחוּ אֶת תְּרוּמָתִי

From each man whose heart is willing shall you take My offering (25:2)

There was once a worthy Jew, Abba Yudin, who lived in Antioch. He gave generously to every charitable cause and especially enjoyed supporting Torah scholars.

And when he gave, he gave with his whole heart.

Then misfortune struck. Abba Yudin lost his wealth and had to sell all of his property and possessions. All that remained was one small field.

Once three noted Sages came to Antioch to collect money for the support of the needy.

When Abba Yudin learned of their arrival, he was disspirited. How he wished that he could give them a generous sum, as he had always done. He returned home early that day, depressed and sorrowful. When his wife saw his expression, she asked in concern, "What is the matter? Are you ill?"

He explained the cause of his low spirits. "Three Sages have arrived in Antioch today. You know how I always welcomed them and gave them a generous gift for their cause. What am I able to give them today? We have nothing left!"

"That is not quite true, dear husband," said his wife, who had always shared her husband's joy in giving to the poor. "We still have one field left. Why don't you go out and sell half of it? The money that you get will make a very generous donation!"

"What a good, virtuous woman you are!" Abba Yudin said admiringly. "Why didn't I think of that? I will do exactly what you said." He ran off to sell half of his field and, as soon as he had the money, he gave it to the three Sages.

The three Sages had already learned about Abba Yudin's hard luck. Yet, they did not refuse his donation but accepted it and blessed him that *Hashem* repay him many times over.

Now Abba Yudin was left with only half a field. One day he went out with his only cow tied to the plow. But as the cow was tugging at the heavy plow it suddenly fell into a pit and broke its leg!

What was Abba Yudin to do now, without a cow and with an unplowed field? Instead of despairing, he went to see what he could do for the poor beast.

When he reached the bottom of the pit, lo and behold, he found a treasure. His cow had stumbled into a pit that contained a chest full of buried gold coins!

He gathered them up and exclaimed with joy, "This is a gift from *Hashem*! How wonderful!"

With the money he had found Abba Yudin was able to buy sheep and cattle, fields and vineyards, houses and servants. He became a rich man, far wealthier than he had ever been before.

Time passed and the Sages came to Antioch again. Upon their arrival they immediately asked about Abba Yudin.

"He is doing fine!" everyone told them. "He is a very prosperous man today. He owns fields and farms, sheep and cattle, anything a person could want! He is richer than he ever was before!"

The Sages were overjoyed to hear that their prayers for him had been answered so quickly. When Abba Yudin learned of their arrival, he rushed to find them and invite them to his home. There he served them with all his graciousness and thanked them for their blessing and gave them a very large donation!

(According to *Midrash Vayikra Rabbah* 5:4)

Gold Coins, Happy Beggars

וְזֹאת הַתְּרוּמָה אֲשֶׁר תִּקְחוּ מֵאִתָּם זָהָב
This is the offering which you shall take from them. Gold... (25:3)

R' Yaakov of Radzimin was such a holy person, so removed from worldly things, that he hardly knew what money looked like. One of his chasidim once came to see him and gave him a few small coins as his *pidyon* gift. To his amazement, the Rebbe gathered up the small pile, examined the coins and shook his head, "There are no shiny ones here. You had better give me some."

"Rebbe!" said the chasid, shocked. "The shiny ones are gold coins! They are worth a lot of money. What use does the Rebbe have for so much money?"

R' Yaakov shrugged his shoulders and explained, "I? I have no use for money, as you know. Everything I get I give directly to the poor. But I do know that they are so happy when I give them those shiny coins."

Treasure Under the Stove

וְעָשׂוּ... מִקְדָּשׁ וְשָׁכַנְתִּי בְּתוֹכָם

And they shall make a sanctuary for Me and I will dwell in their midst (25:8)

The Divine Presence will rest in the Mikdash and also 'within them' — within each and every Jew.

(Writings)

The Rebbe, Reb Bunim, had a special story that he always told chasidim who came to him for the first time:

There was once an impoverished man by the name of Reb Isaac ben Yakil of Cracow. He lived in poverty for many years, not knowing where his next crust of bread would come from. Still, Reb Isaac had implicit faith that *Hashem* would not let him starve and that some day He would free him of his suffering.

One night Reb Isaac had a curious dream. In it, he was told to go to Prague where, if he dug under a bridge, he would find a buried treasure of great value. It would make him a rich man!

At first Reb Isaac paid no attention to the dream, thinking it to be mere wishful thinking. Who did not dream of becoming rich? But when the dream repeated itself in the nights which followed, he began to have second thoughts. Perhaps there was something to it after all.

The next morning, when he arose, he made up his mind to go to Prague and see what would happen. It was a long, tiring journey but he finally reached his destination only to find that the bridge he was looking for was right near the royal palace and was heavily guarded.

Soldiers stood there day and night, marching back and forth, alert to any sign of danger or any unusual activity. It was out of the question to begin digging under that bridge, Reb Isaac knew. Still, he did not lose hope. If he had come all this way, he would stay here a bit more and see if anything new developed.

Each day Reb Isaac visited the bridge until he became a familiar figure to the guards. And soon his presence aroused their curiosity. What did he want here? One morning the head of the guards spoke to him and asked, "What is it that you are looking for here at the bridge? Are you waiting for someone or something?"

Reb Isaac knew that he could not put him off with some lame answer. He told him the truth about the dream he had had back home in Cracow and of the treasure waiting for him under the bridge.

The head of the guards listened, then threw back his head and laughed heartily. "You came all this way just because of a silly dream? What a fool to believe in idle dreams! If I believed in dreams, I would be in Cracow now myself! I had a dream that there was a certain Jew, Reb Isaac ben Yakil, under whose stove there was a buried treasure. But do you think that I am such a fool as to go there on a wild goose chase? Not I!"

While the guard was laughing, Reb Isaac had already turned away. He was at the coach station in minutes, buying a ticket for the first coach leaving for Cracow. Now he knew where he had to look.

When he arrived home he shoved the iron stove away and began digging at the hard-packed dirt floor. Sure

enough, after some effort he uncovered a chest of gold coins. He took the money and built a magnificent synagogue with it which bore his name, "Reb Isaac ben Yakil's Shul". With the rest, he built himself a home, furnished it well and lived happily ever after.

When new chasidim heard Reb Bunim tell this tale, they would understand his point. He meant to say that one did not always find what one wanted by seeking afar, by traveling to some distant chasidic court. True spiritual treasure could be acquired by intense self-effort, and by devout prayer. Even near home one could find what one was seeking, G-dly worship, holiness, and high spiritual levels.

Blaze the Trail

וְעָשִׂיתָ עָלָיו זֵר זָהָב סָבִיב

And you shall make for it a golden border all around (25:11)

This refers to the crown of Torah.

(Rashi)

This teaches you to honor Torah scholars.

(Holy writings)

It was a frosty night. The entire city was covered over with a blanket of thick white snow. The cold bit into one's bones.

It was at that hour just before dawn when the night is at its coldest. At this inhospitable hour the scholars of Horodna were just getting up to go to the *beis medrash* for their daily pre-dawn lesson.

How surprised they were to see a figure dancing in the knee-high snow. He was bundled up in warm fur but his teeth were chattering nevertheless. Whatever was this person up to at this hour? As they approached, they could hear him muttering, "*Leshem mitzvah* — this is for the sake of a *mitzvah*!"

More and more puzzling! Who was this man? Had he gone out of his mind? Dancing in the snow in the middle of the night? They drew nearer, determined to clear up the mystery.

They approached and were finally able to identify the face concealed behind the high fur collar. It was R' Nachum of Horodna. They cried out in alarm, "What is the matter, R' Nachum?"

R' Nachum lowered his eyes, ashamed at having been caught in the act. Sheepishly, he explained what he had been doing.

"It is almost morning. Soon dozens of *cheder* children will be rushing off to learn Torah. They are not very strong. Nor are they well protected from the cold. Their families cannot afford warm coats for them; their shoes are worn and torn. I am afraid that Jewish children might catch cold, if they have to struggle against the freezing elements. I thought that I, who had a warm fur coat, could blaze the way for them."

The Misguided Gift

וְנָתַתָּ עַל הַשֻּׁלְחָן לֶחֶם פָּנִים

And you shall put the show bread upon the Shulchan (25:30)

A Marrano managed to escape from Portugal during the Inquisition and reached Tsefas in *Eretz Yisrael*. Shortly after his arrival he happened to be in *beis knesses* one *Shabbos* afternoon when the rabbi spoke about the sacrifice of the twelve loaves, the *lechem hapanim* that the *kohanim* brought in the *Beis Hamikdash* each week. This, he explained, served to bring *Hashem*'s blessing upon the Jewish people throughout that week.

In reminding his congregation that, alas, the *Beis Hamikdash* was no longer standing, the rabbi heaved a deep sigh, saying, "And now we have nothing upon which *Hashem*'s bounty can rest, through which the Jewish people can receive the Heavenly blessing."

The Marrano returned home and, in all innocence, told his wife that from now on she was to prepare two loaves from flour sifted thirteen times, as it had been in the *Beis Hamikdash*. She was to knead the dough in purity and bake it well. He wanted these loaves as a sacrifice for *Hashem*, just as it had been offered in the *Beis Hamikdash*.

The wife dutifully did exactly as her husband had said. Each Friday she would bake fresh loaves according to his precise instructions. When they were ready, the Marrano would bring them to the synagogue, walk up to the *aron kodesh* and pray that his sacrifice be accepted with favor. Then, after his heartfelt plea, he would place the two loaves inside and leave.

The *shammash* of the synagogue was more than happy to receive this offering. Friday after Friday, when he went to make last-minute preparations in the synagogue, he would find the two loaves, redolent and tempting, nestled behind the velvet curtain. He did not ask who had brought them. He did not care. He was happy enough for this small gift which made such a difference to his *Shabbos*.

When the Marrano returned in the evening, together with the rest of the worshippers, he always noticed, to his satisfaction, that the loaves had disappeared. "Straight to heaven," he imagined in his innocence. And when he returned home he would tell his good wife that her efforts had been blessed and urge her to be as careful the following week so as not to displease *Hashem.*

Week after week this practice went on, the Marrano delivering his offering and the *shammash* accepting it, neither knowing of the other.

One time, however, the rabbi himself came to the *beis knesses.* He wished to practice his sermon by delivering it from the *bimah* that week. He was standing there when the Marrano entered with the two hot loaves tucked under his arms. Without even noticing that there was anyone else present, he went over to the ark, as usual, and poured out the feelings of his heart, begging *Hashem* to accept his gift. Then he lovingly placed the two loaves behind the curtain and went down the three steps.

The rabbi had not breathed a word all this time. He was deeply shocked and too stunned to act. Besides, he was curious to see what was going on. When the Jew had set down his gift and was about to leave, the rabbi finally came to his senses and thundered at him,

"Fool! Idiot! Do you really think that G-d eats and drinks? That He accepts your loaves? It must be the *shammash* who is glad for the extra bread on his table. What simplicity! Do you know that it is a terrible sin to attribute human traits to *Hashem* and to imagine that He actually eats? How stupid can you be?!"

The rabbi had just finished his tirade when the *shammash* entered to fetch his weekly loaves. Not noticing the two men, he walked over to the ark and lifted the curtain. The rabbi stopped him.

"Thank this man here for your fresh *challos,*" he said.

א ב ג ד ה
ו ז ח ט י

"He has been bringing them here each week."

The *shammash* murmured his thanks in confused, garbled tones.

The rabbi now looked back at the Marrano to see his reaction to the revelation that it was the *shammash*, after all, who took his precious gift of loaves. The man had turned a pasty white. Tears were streaming down his cheeks. "Forgive me," he said to the rabbi. "I made a mistake. I did not know. I misunderstood your sermon about the *lechem hapanim*. I wanted to do a *mitzvah*... that was all! But instead I have committed a terrible sin."

The tears came gushing forth, faster and faster, as he realized that his good intentions had not only been for naught, but had even been evil! Suddenly, a fourth person burst in on this scene: a messenger from the Ari Hakadosh who lived in Tsefas at the time. The messenger said to the rabbi, "Return home and prepare your family for your death. Tomorrow at the hour which you were to give your sermon in the synagogue — you will die! This has been decreed by heaven!"

The rabbi was startled. Out of the blue? He rushed out of the room and ran as fast as he could, straight to the Ari.

"What is the meaning of that announcement? What have I done to deserve such a sudden death?"

The Ari explained, "You spoiled a source of great satisfaction to *Hashem*. Know, that ever since the *Beis Hamikdash* was destroyed, never did our Heavenly Father derive such pleasure from a human gift as He did from the simple, wholesome deed of that Marrano when he brought his two loaves, thinking that *Hashem* actually accepted and ate them. But, since by your anger you interfered and brought this sacrifice to an end, you have been sentenced to death. There is no hope to reverse that decree!"

The rabbi returned to his home, crushed. He told his family exactly what had happened and what the Ari had said.

The following day, just at the time of the usual sermon, the rabbi returned his soul to his Maker.

Outsmarting a Wise Man

וְה׳ נָתַן חָכְמָה לִשְׁלֹמֹה

And Hashem gave wisdom to Shlomo

(Haftorah Parashas Terumah, Melachim I, 5)

When King Shlomo was finally told that he could begin building the *Beis Hamikdash,* he was overjoyed and laid grand plans. He wanted it to be the most magnificent building that had ever existed. Knowing that excellent artists and craftsmen were to be had in Egypt, he sent a message to Pharaoh Necho asking that he send his best workers. "I will pay them generously," he promised.

Pharaoh knew that he could not refuse this mighty king. But he wished to outsmart him. He sent for his wisest astrologers and asked them, "Which of all the talented people in Egypt are fated to die within the year?"

The astrologers made their calculations and gave a list

to the king. These were the men Pharaoh sent to King Shlomo.

But Shlomo, wisest of all men, knew through his divine intuition the trick that Pharaoh had played on him. He provided each Egyptian craftsman with a set of shrouds, in which dead men are buried, and sent them right back to Egypt with the following message for their king: "Have you no shrouds in Egypt to bury your dead? Here, take these together with your ill-fated men!"

When he saw this, Pharaoh understood that he had chosen the wrong person to fool. Shlomo had lived up to his reputation and fame as being the wisest man on earth. He also understood now why *Hashem* had chosen him to build His house of glory!

(According to *Midrash Bamidbar Rabbah 19*)

פָּרָשַׁת תְּצַוֶּה

Parashas Tetzaveh

The Mitzvah of Silence

וְאַתָּה תְּדַבֵּר אֶל כָּל חַכְמֵי לֵב

And you shall speak to all the wise of heart (28:3)

One evening the Vishnitzer Rebbe, R' Yisrael, was taking his usual walk, accompanied by his loyal *shammash*. This time, however, they ventured further than ever before, reaching the suburbs which housed the wealthier inhabitants. The homes here were spacious and luxurious, surrounded by well-tended lawns. They were the homes of Jews who had become estranged from Judaism.

The *shammash* could not help wondering what business the Rebbe had in this neighborhood. Certainly, none of his chasidim lived here. How much greater was his astonishment when the Rebbe stopped in front of one of the houses, the home of a well-known banker.

The Rebbe strode up and knocked at the door. The *shammash* followed dutifully behind, but could not help wondering what the Rebbe was doing.

If the *shammash* was surprised, how much more so was the banker who opened the door himself and saw the Vishnitzer Rebbe standing before him. He rushed forward and greeted him with a hearty yet respectful "*shalom aleichem*!" He ushered him into his living room and showed him to the most comfortable chair. Then he sat down himself. What business could the Rebbe possibly have with him?

The banker waited and the *shammash* waited. And the Rebbe waited. He sat there, not uttering a single word, just sitting there thoughtfully. After a long silence, the banker made a gesture to capture the *shammash*'s attention, then whispered to him, "What does the Rebbe want from me?" The *shammash* whispered back, "I don't know myself."

This strange silence continued for a few more minutes. Finally, the Rebbe stood up and, without having said a single word, was about to leave the house.

The banker jumped up to see his visitor to the door. The Rebbe still had not revealed the purpose of this strange visit. And yet he was on his way home, without having spoken a single word. The banker followed behind the Rebbe, still not daring to speak, to ask the one question that puzzled him. He followed the Rebbe all the way to his home. When the Rebbe stood on the threshold with one foot already in the house, the banker could no longer contain his curiosity and blurted out, "Please excuse me for my question. While you were in my house, it would have been impolite for me to ask why I was privileged with such an honored visit. But here, at your own doorstep, I must venture to ask that question. Why did the Rebbe come to me tonight?"

The Rebbe finally broke his silence by saying, "I came to you tonight to fulfill a commandment. Thank G-d, I have fulfilled it!"

R' Yisrael's strange reply puzzled the banker even more

and he could not help asking, "What *mitzvah* could the Rebbe possibly have fulfilled by sitting in my house and maintaining silence?!"

The Rebbe explained, "Our Sages taught us that just as it is a *mitzvah* to say something that will be heeded, so is it a *mitzvah* to refrain from saying that which will not be listened to. If I had sat in my home and you, in yours, I would not have accomplished anything; you would not have been aware that I refrained from telling you something that you would not heed!"

The banker's curiosity was not satisfied. He still wanted to know what the Rebbe had *not* said! "Perhaps, if the Rebbe said that thing to me, I might listen after all?" he suggested.

The Rebbe shook his head sadly. "No, I am certain that you would not listen."

The banker was piqued. He begged and pleaded that the Rebbe mention what he had in mind, but the Rebbe was adamant. It was forbidden to say something that would not be heard.

The more he urged, the more strongly the Rebbe refused. Finally, however, the Rebbe could not withstand his earnest pleading and said, "You want to know what I had in mind? Very well. There is a widow who owes your bank a large payment on a mortgage. She does not have any money to pay it. In a few days the bank will foreclose the mortgage and put her home up for sale, evict her and leave her and her fatherless orphans without a roof over their heads. I really would have liked to ask you to cancel this widow's debt, but I did not, knowing that there was no chance of your listening to me. When I came here tonight it was *not* to ask you but at least to fulfill my obligation of not saying something which would not have been heeded. Now you understand."

The banker heard the Rebbe's request and reacted with surprise, "But how could I possibly cancel a woman's debt on a mortgage payment? It simply is not done! If it were a personal debt to me, that would be an entirely different matter but this is bank business, a default of payment to a public institution! I am not the owner of this bank, only its manager! Besides, you are talking about an enormous sum!"

The Rebbe smiled a wise, sad smile. "I was right, then, wasn't I, in saying that you would not listen to what I said? I should not have said it altogether."

The Rebbe turned away from the banker and entered his house, followed by his *shammash*. The rich banker remained standing, stranded on the threshold. He stood there for a moment, then turned to leave. But on the way home he was bothered by many thoughts. The outcome of this story, as you may guess, is that the widow's home was not sold.

To Be a Kohen

וְאֵלֶּה הַבְּגָדִים אֲשֶׁר יַעֲשׂוּ

These are the garments which they shall make (28:4)

Once a Roman passed by a classroom where Jewish children were studying *chumash*. He overheard the teacher reading from the Torah, describing the magnificent clothing which the *Kohen Gadol* wore — the fine embroidered linen, the gold decorations, and a breastplate of gleaming gems. Gold, royal purple, indigo blue, gold chains, precious stones — all of these captured his fancy and lit up his imagination. He rushed into the classroom and asked the teacher,"The clothing that you just described — for whom is it intended? Who wears such glorious apparel?"

The teacher replied, "They are for the *Kohen Gadol*!"

The Roman thought, "I will tell the Jews that I am willing to convert on condition that I become a *Kohen Gadol* and wear those magnificent garments!"

He turned towards Shammai's *beis midrash*. He knew that Shammai was a greatly respected Jewish Sage. Striding confidently right up to Shammai, he announced, "I have come to convert to Judaism. I agree to accept your religion, but only on one condition: that you appoint me as *Kohen Gadol* in your Temple."

Shammai thought that he was ridiculing him. What a crazy notion! He had no time to waste on foolishness like this. He chased the Roman out of his study hall in great anger.

The Roman was not discouraged. He next visited Hillel, another Sage, whose patience everyone praised so highly. He walked in and said, "I wish to convert, but only under one condition: that you appoint me *Kohen Gadol* in your Temple."

Hillel saw that he was serious. Apparently, he was not aware that only men who are born *kohanim* are eligible to become *Kohen Gadol*. He understood that the Roman thought that, just like anyone could become king, so could anyone eventually become *Kohen Gadol*, if he proved worthy enough.

Patiently and kindly he said, "Surely, you realize that,

before becoming a king, one must first learn many things: martial arts, diplomacy, court behavior and so forth. The same applies to the office of *Kohen Gadol.* He must first study Torah in order to know his duties and privileges and so forth."

The Roman was able to understand this well enough. "That is very logical, I must admit. Very well, I will begin by studying Torah." And he began to learn Torah from the very beginning. He applied himself diligently and seriously.

When he came to *Chumash Bamidbar* he learned that only the *leviim* were permitted to handle the holy vessels of the *Mishkan.* The Torah said: "And the stranger who draws close shall die."

Alarmed, he ran to Hillel and asked, "To whom does this apply?"

Hillel answered, "These words apply to everyone, even to King David himself. Anyone who is not a *levi* is forbidden from serving in the *Beis Hamikdash* and even from touching its holy vessels."

The Roman began thinking aloud, "If this applies to all Jews who are the descendants of the Patriarchs Avraham, Yitzchak and Yaakov, *Hashem*'s chosen people, how much more would they apply to one not born a Jew! How can I, who have just joined this nation and who does not have the parental merit of their forefathers — even dream of approaching the holy vessels of the *Beis Hamikdash* and not expect to die?! I am neither a *kohen* nor a *levi.* What a fool I was to have ever embraced such a thought?"

He now returned to Shammai and asked, "Why did you reject me so hastily? Why did you not explain that I did not possibly have a chance of becoming a *Kohen Gadol*? Why didn't you tell me I was talking foolishness?"

He stalked out and returned to Hillel. "How grateful I am to you!" he said. "May *Hashem* heap blessings upon your head. I thank you most heartily for having drawn me close to Judaism.

(According to Tractate *Shabbos 31*)

Gold Inlay are Her Garments

וְעָשִׂיתָ מִשְׁבְּצֹת זָהָב

And you shall make an inlay of gold (28:13)

There was once a woman called Kimchis who had seven sons, all of whom served as *Kohanim Gedolim*.

Curious to learn her secret so that she could serve as a shining example to others, the Sages paid her a visit. They asked her, "Why did you deserve to see all your seven sons serve as *Kohanim Gedolim?*"

She replied, "Throughout my married life, I never bared my head even to the four walls of my own house!" This was how careful she was with regard to the laws of *tzniyus*, modesty.

Upon hearing this, the Sages applied the following verse to her,, "A princess' greatest prestige is from within — gold inlay is her raiment." Whoever is as cautious and careful about her personal self-respect as is a princess, behaves with inner modesty and does not thrust herself forward, is rewarded with clothing of gold inlay — sons who shall serve as *Kohanim Gedolim* and wear the golden garments of the *Kohen Gadol.*

(According to *Midrash Vayikra Rabbah 20:11*)

The Silence that Saved

וְנִשְׁמַע קוֹלוֹ בְּבֹאוֹ אֶל הַקֹּדֶשׁ

And his sound will be heard when he comes to the Sanctuary (28:35)

The kohen's tunic (me'il) atones for the sin of slander. Hashem said: Let that which makes sound come and atone for the sins of sound.

(Tractate Arachin 16a)

For many years the Vilna Gaon remained secluded among his holy books. One time, however, he decided that he must go into a self-imposed exile and travel from city to city. During this period he would hire a Jewish wagoner to drive him around. The Vilna Gaon did not waste time, even while traveling. He was always learning and would become so absorbed that he never even had an inkling of what was going on around him.

Once, the horse strayed off the path, attracted by the garden of some gentile farmer. The horse greedily began devouring the luscious carrots and beets and even the pretty flowers.

As soon as the wagoner saw what was happening, he jumped off the wagon and ran to hide among the roadside bushes, knowing that it would not be long before the farmer or his wife came out and discovered the damage. He abandoned his distinguished passenger, R' Eliyahu, to his fate.

His fears were not unfounded. Within a few moments a husky gentile burst out of the house, heading straight for the wagon. He peered inside the wagon and saw the distinguished Jew seated inside. Having no one else to blame for the damage to his garden, he pounced upon this unwitting victim.

Suddenly, this brilliant scholar was wrenched from his world of the spirit by a barrage of blows. He had no idea why he was being beaten, but he did not protest either. This provoked the gentile even further and he began striking with all his might, blow after blow. "Why do you pretend to be so innocent?!" he thundered. "You know, well enough, that your horse ruined my entire vegetable garden and my flower beds as well! Don't you have anything to say for yourself? I bet you even did it on purpose. Well, I will make you pay for this, you can be sure!"

At least now the Gaon knew what it was all about! How could he convince the farmer that it was all a mistake, that it was his wagoner's fault? He was about to point out where the wagoner was hiding, (he had caught a glimpse of him) when suddenly he realized,

"I cannot inform on a Jew! I must not speak against a fellow Jew!"

The Gaon was silent. He let the gentile pour his blows upon his body, but would not open his mouth. In later years he would recall this incident and thank *Hashem* for having saved him from a sin at the crucial moment. He did not think at all of the murderous blows he had received. No! All he remembered about that incident was the sin that he had almost committed... a sin, for which, if he had indeed transgressed, he would never have forgiven himself. A sin for which all of his vast Torah knowledge would not have been able to save him from punishment.

The Feast of Thanks-giving

וְאִם נִכְלְמוּ מִכֹּל אֲשֶׁר עָשׂוּ

And if they be ashamed of all they have done?
(Haftorah Parashas Tetzaveh, Yechezkel 43)

R' Mendel of Premislan did not believe in punishing himself by fasting or other self-torments. "The human body," he used to say, "is the handiwork of *Hashem*. What right do I have to punish or persecute it?" But when he was visited by suffering, he rejoiced and welcomed it. "Suffering cleanses and purifies the body from sin. I am not responsible for bringing this on, that is why I welcome it."

Once, R' Mendel invited a large number of his followers and friends to a feast of thanks-giving. Everyone came but could not help asking, "What is the reason for this celebration?"

The Rebbe explained, 'Today someone embarrassed me in public."

The reply left them even more puzzled.

R' Mendel explained. "When a person falls ill and recovers, does he not hold a feast of thanks? Why? Because the suffering he felt through his illness served to cleanse and erase his account of sins. His recovery was a sign from Heaven that his atonement had been accepted. Our Sages also said that one who was publicly shamed has his record of sins wiped clean. Since this is so, should I not rejoice? Should I not also hold a feast of thanks-giving?"

פָּרָשַׁת כִּי תִשָּׂא

Parashas Ki Sisa

The Waves Drew Him Up

וְנָתְנוּ אִישׁ כֹּפֶר נַפְשׁוֹ

Each man shall give a ransom for his soul (30:12)

A worthy Jew, known for his charity, once took a sea voyage. While he was in mid-ocean a sudden storm arose and the ship sank, with all of its passengers aboard.

R' Akiva happened to witness the tragedy and went to court to testify to the man's death. Thus his widow would be able to remarry. But before the court was able to question him thoroughly and take his testimony as final, someone burst into the court. It was the 'dead' man himself!

"What happened?" R' Akiva asked him, hardly believing his eyes. "Didn't I see you drowning?"

"Yes, you did!" the man agreed.

"Then what happened? How were you saved when the ship sank and all the passengers drowned?"

"I was saved," the man replied, "because of the charity which I had given."

"How do you know that?" R' Akiva asked.

He said, "When I sank down to the bottom of the sea, I heard the crashing of water all around me. One wave said to another, 'Let us rush to that man and lift him up for he gave charity throughout his life.' And that is what happened. The waves themselves drew me up and brought me to land. Thus I was saved."

When R' Akiva heard this he said, "Blessed is *Hashem*, the G-d of Israel, Who chose the Torah and its Sages, for the Torah and the Torah Sages exist forever. As it says, 'Cast your bread upon the water... for with the passing of days you shall surely find it!' It also says, 'And charity shall save from death!"

(According to *Midrash Koheles Rabbah 11,1*)

The Peasant's Donation

לַחְשֹׁב מַחֲשָׁבֹת לַעֲשׂוֹת בַּזָּהָב

To work in gold (31:4)

The people revered R' Chaim of Volozhin not only for his Torah scholarship, but for his insight. He would often be called upon to smooth the differences between the two parties of a quarrel.

The following story illustrates this cleverness and insight:

When R' Chaim founded the Yeshivah of Volozhin he delegated a man to raise money for its maintenance. Among the contributors was a villager, who gave generously and with a willing heart.

With time the sum of monies which had been collected

dwindled and the collector was forced to travel and gather more funds. Before he set out on his trip, he requested a new set of fine clothes, so as to make a good impression upon his prospective contributors. A suit was ordered. When it was ready, the *meshulach* also requested a horse and carriage. This, he said, would save him much time and would also make a fine impression on people. This, too, was granted.

The *meshulach* left Volozhin looking like a new man, like a prosperous person himself. In time, he paid a visit to the villager who had previously given generously. To his great surprise, the man refused to give him a penny this time. The *meshulach* tried all kinds of arguments but nothing helped. The man kept his purse strings tightly shut and was very cold towards him.

Terribly disappointed, the collector returned to R' Chaim and told him what had happened. R' Chaim listened and decided to pay the villager a visit.

The man received the *rosh yeshivah* with the honor and respect that was his due. After the usual pleasantries, R' Chaim finally came to the point of his visit. "Why have you stopped supporting the Volozhiner Yeshivah?" he asked.

The villager explained: "I will tell you the truth, Rebbe. Up to now, I naively thought that the money I gave went directly towards supporting the *yeshivah* itself and its needy students. For that I gave willingly, for I greatly respect Torah study and certainly wish to have a portion in it. But when your fundraiser came this time, all decked out in a fancy tailored suit and a splendid carriage, I thought that the money I gave would be going towards support of these unnecessary trappings. I do not want my money wasted on such frills."

R' Chaim replied, "You have a point, my friend. But I would like you to see things in their true light. Surely you are familiar with the verse that says of Bezalel, who supervised the work of the *Mishkan,* 'And I filled him with the spirit of *Hashem,* with knowledge, intelligence and wisdom to know... to do creative work... in gold and silver and copper.' One would assume that all the contributors for the *Mishkan* gave their contributions for the Holy of Holies. But, in fact, the gifts were used for other purposes as well. It was Bezalel's special genius to intuitively know the inner thoughts and intentions of each donor and to measure his sincerity. He was able to know whether a donor gave his offer purely for the sake of Heaven, without secondary thoughts of honor and prestige, and to use the gifts accordingly.

"When a person gave his offering with pure intention, to enhance the House of *Hashem,* then Bezalel used the gold and silver for the Holy of Holies. If, however, a person had additional thoughts, and thought the gifts would make him important in the eyes of others, then they were used for other parts of the *Mishkan.*

"The same applies here," R' Chaim explained. The money that you give is intended to support Torah directly. Your intentions and thoughts are pure, *leshem shamayim,* for Heaven's sake alone. Rest assured that it goes for that purpose alone. There are others who give to the *yeshivah* both for the sake of Torah and for their good name, for their reputation. Their money goes to keep up appearances too, for the magnificent coach and finely tailored clothing of our *meshulach,* which is also important in its own right. Those who only give to keep up their own good name — their money goes for the horse's fodder and the repair and upkeep of the coach."

The villager was all smiles. "Oh! Rebbe! How glad I am that you explained this to me. To tell the truth, it hurt me very much to have to refuse the collector for I truly believe in the *yeshivah* and greatly want a share in its great work. Now that you assure me that my money will go for that alone, I feel so much better."

And he gave R' Chaim his donation with renewed joy.

Plans for One Egg

לַחְשֹׁב מַחֲשָׁבוֹת לַעֲשׂוֹת

To think thoughts and to work (31:4)

With the advent of the *Yomim Noraim,* High Holy Days, R' Chaim of Sanz used to tell his chasidim the following parable in order to admonish them:

There was once a poor widow who had many young children to feed but all she owned was a single egg, a gift from a kind neighbor. Cradling this precious possession carefully in her hand, she began daydreaming:

I will take this egg to my neighbor who has a chicken coop and ask her if I can put it under a hen so that she can sit on it until it hatches. Then out will burst a fluffy bundle of yellow feathers, my own little chick. It will raise this chick until it becomes a hen. In time, this hen will begin laying eggs of its own. I will not eat the eggs, but will let them hatch until I have a great many chicks tumbling all over my yard! What a lovely sight that will be. And these too will begin laying until I have enough to fill a chicken coop. When they will be too much to handle, I will take them to town and sell them at the market. With the money they fetch, I will be able to buy myself a fine calf which will grow up into a cow. Who knows, before long I will have an entire herd of cattle! I will sell them and be rich! I will be able to buy a house and a field, hire servants, clothe my children in velvet and silk...

BOOM! CRASH! SPLATTER!

While she had been busy spinning dreams of her golden future, about houses and orchards, vineyards and servants, the egg had slipped from her hand and fell to the ground where it shattered — and with it, her beautiful dreams.

"The moral should be clear to you all," the Rebbe would conclude. "It applies to many Jews who make grandiose plans during the month of *Elul* and the Ten Days of Penitence to improve all of their ways. They resolve to observe all of the *mitzvos* most carefully, to abstain from *lashon hara,* to learn more and more and so forth — fine, admirable resolutions. But what happens then? The bubble bursts. The fine resolutions crash to the ground and nothing is left. All the golden ideas explode in the face of gray reality which is left empty of *mitzvos* and good deeds.

The Rabbi's Wisdom

וּבְלֵב כָּל חֲכַם־לֵב נָתַתִּי חָכְמָה

And in the heart of all that are wise-hearted I have placed wisdom (31:6)

A Jew from Bialystock once had to travel far from home for business reasons. His family did not hear any word from him for a long time. When they finally received a letter, they were very puzzled and worried. It read:

"I am about to sign a contract on an important business deal but I need a large sum of money. Please forward it to me at once." The man's signature, however, even though in his own handwriting, was odd. He had signed his name with the addition of "*Segal*" which denotes that a person is a *Levi* — and he was not a *Levi*!

The family was thoroughly bewildered. Why would a man sign himself as a *Levi* when he was not one? They finally decided to go to a wise rabbi who might be able to throw light on this riddle.

They went to R' Moshe Ze'ev, *av beis din* of Tiktin for advice. He read the letter and then said urgently, "Quick. Gather a group of armed men and go to the address that appears here. A man's life is in danger! It is a matter of life and death."

R' Moshe Ze'ev explained, "The name '*Segal*' which appears in the signature is formed by the first letters of the words '*sakana gedolah li*' — I am threatened by a grave danger!" And now hurry before you are too late!"

A group of armed men went off immediately. The rabbi had been right! The man's life had been in danger. He had been kidnapped for ransom and would have been killed as soon as the money had arrived. The Rabbi had interpreted the hidden message correctly and the man was saved.

The Loss and the Gain

לַעֲשׂוֹת אֶת הַשַּׁבָּת לְדֹרֹתָם
To make Shabbos for all their generations (31:16)

Reb Yisrael Isser was one of Cracow's most prominent Jews. He owned a flourishing dry goods shop which stocked the best linens, softest velvets, most shimmering silks and the finest wools. Customers flocked to him, not only for his superior goods but because he was scrupulously honest. Fine goods and fine character were the secrets of his success.

Reb Yisrael Isser had an iron rule. He would shut his shop on Friday at noon. Exactly when the town clock struck twelve, he would kindly ask his customers to leave. He would lock up and head straight for home to prepare for *Shabbos.*

One Friday morning a distinguished cloth merchant came to Reb Yisrael Isser's shop with a long list of merchandise which he needed. The shopkeeper began taking bolt after bolt down from the shelves, unrolling them out on the counter for display. Soon the surface was piled with goods. Some were rejected, but many were to be cut to the customer's specifications.

The clock struck twelve noon. Reb Yisrael turned to his customer and spoke kindly, but firmly, "I am afraid that it is closing time. We will have to continue another time."

"What do you mean, 'closing time'? It is only twelve

o'clock. Who in their right mind closes his shop so early? And when you have such a good customer as myself. Why, just look around, I have selected a good portion of your shop here. It would be ridiculous for you to chase me away now. Besides, I cannot possibly come back next week. I have a large order from a tailor who sews for the nobility. If I disappoint him, he will go to another dealer."

Reb Yisrael Isser shrugged his shoulders and began jingling his keys. He edged towards the door. "That is my rule. I do not break it for anyone."

"And what if I take my business elsewhere?"

"That is your own business. It would be a great loss to me, I cannot deny that. But I have no choice. I will not keep my shop open after noon on Fridays, no matter how great the loss. And now will you please step this way..." He had his hand on the customer's arm and was showing him out. Reb Yisrael Isser did not even bother to replace the merchandise and tidy up the shelves. He left, together with the customer, and went home.

His loss was a considerable one. He would have made a great profit from that sale. He had also lost a customer, one of his best. And yet, the *Shabbos* had been dearer to him than any sum of money. Reb Yisrael Isser's sacrifice made a great impression in Heaven. The heavenly court decided to reward him with a gift far more precious than money. Reb Yisrael Isser was given a son, a very special one. When little Moshe grew up he became one of the greatest *poskim, halachic* authorities, which our people have known. And the name by which he was known and always referred to, incorporated that of his father: he was the famous Ramo — R' Moshe Isserlish (Isser's son).

Truly a gain well worth the loss!

Worse Than Bitul Torah?

אִם תִּשָּׂא חַטָּאתָם וְאִם אַיִן מְחֵנִי נָא

If You forgive their sin, and if not, erase me (32:32)

R' Yehudah Hanasi, or Rebbe, as he was fondly called, was once sitting in the *beis midrash*, teaching Torah. Suddenly, his nostrils caught the offensive smell of garlic coming from one of the students.

"Whoever has eaten garlic recently is requested to step out!" he said.

R' Chiya got up and left. Since R' Chiya was one of the most respected disciples, when he arose he was followed by the rest of the students present. The *beis midrash* was silent.

On the following day R' Shimon, Rebbe's son, met R' Chiya and challenged him, "Are you the one who hurt my father yesterday?" What he meant was — Are you the one who caused my father pain because of *bitul Torah*, neglect from learning Torah?

R' Chiya defended himself, "You are right that wasting time from Torah study is a serious sin. But, humiliating a Jew is even worse! Let me tell you, I am not the one who ate the garlic. But I thought to myself: "It is better that I cause all of those students to miss out on a Torah lesson rather than that even one of them be embarrassed. That is why I got up and left the room. Then the others followed in my footsteps."

(Adapted from Tractate *Sanhedrin 13a*)

Public Demand

וְדִבֶּר ה׳ אֶל מֹשֶׁה... וְשָׁב אֶל הַמַּחֲנֶה

And Hashem spoke to Moshe... and he returned to the camp
(33:11)

Hashem told Moshe to return to the camp. He said: I am angry and you are angry. Who then will draw them (the Jews) close to me?

(Rashi)

A huge crowd had gathered at the train station and still more were streaming from all directions. The platform was packed with people. They filled the station, they spilled out of the doors and surrounded the building.

"What was going on? What were all those Jews doing here?" one station attendant asked of another.

"Some important person is about to pass through on the train to Vienna. He is a great rabbi. People are flocking just to get a glimpse of him," someone explained.

"Only passing through? He is not even stopping here? Who could it be? Who would deserve such respect?"

It was the Chafetz Chaim, on his way to the first convention of Agudas Yisrael in Vienna. Jews, who for years had been hearing of his saintliness and greatness, wished, at least once in their lifetime, to see him with their own eyes. They wanted to be able to tell their grandchildren that they had actually beheld him.

When the train pulled into the station, a delegation of worthy Jews entered the Chafetz Chaim's compartment and asked him to please go out to the people who had gathered in multitudes to see him. The Chafetz Chaim refused.

"All my life," he said, "I have fled from honor. Do you expect that now, when I am old, I should change my practice? It is out of the question. Don't you know that in the World-to-Come all the pleasure which a person enjoys in this world is not deducted from his ultimate reward for the *mitzvos* which he performed. But the pleasure he derives from honor given to him — which is not even tangible — that is deducted from his record!"

The Chafetz Chaim was not the only *gadol* traveling to Vienna. R' Meir Dan Plotzki, rabbi of Ostrow, was also in the compartment. He demurred and said, "In my humble opinion, I think that one should not ignore the request of so many good Jews gathered at this station. I would imagine that it is worthwhile forfeiting a little bit of one's *olam haba* in order to satisfy them. Besides, I doubt if one really does lose anything."

"Enough!" said the Chafetz Chaim good-naturedly. "Your first reason was enough for me — respect another person and to honor his request." Without another word he rose, went over to the window so that everyone could see him, and blessed the crowds.

The journey to Vienna was a long one with many stops in between. At every stop Jews gathered to catch a glimpse of the Chafetz Chaim. But the long trip sapped his strength and he asked that the doors of the compartment be shut and the window shades lowered, so that he could take a nap and not present himself to further throngs of people.

The window shades were lowered. However, after a brief lapse of time the conductor came rushing into the Chafetz Chaim's compartment. "All the passengers here must transfer to another coach. A fire has broken out and it is dangerous to remain here."

The Chafetz Chaim heard this and, turning to his companions, said, "Do you see the power of the public? I have no choice but to go out to the people anyway, and honor their wishes."

The Rescue

וְרִחַמְתִּי אֶת אֲשֶׁר אֲרַחֵם

And I shall show mercy to whom I will show mercy (33:19)

Hashem said: I give measure for measure. I take pity on whoever is prepared to say to his fellow man, "I pity you."

(Sefer Razin d'Oraysah)

The skies were cloudless. The sun sent out friendly warm rays to caress the still waters. Everyone, even the seasoned sailors, predicted smooth sailing.

The first few days of the journey were, indeed, pleasant. Suddenly, when the ship was on the high seas, a storm struck.

Winds howled and raged; lightning flashed; thunder roared; rain beat down in torrents. The ship was tossed about like a nutshell. Then, a huge wave lifted it onto a reef. Now, the highest waves could not reach it, the fiercest winds could not budge it.

However, on board they were more fearful than before.

They were safe from the storm but they were stranded and would starve to death. To leave the boat was out of the question, even after the storm passed. For the waters were infested with sharks and other dangerous creatures. And where could they go? Who would find them? Ships did not pass by often. They had been saved from the tempest only to fall into even greater dangers.

All, passengers and sailors alike, gathered together and held a conference. The first thing they decided was to pool all the food and divide everything up equally. This praiseworthy act made a deep impression in Heaven. *Hashem* inspired them and they thought of a solution to their dilemma.

Among the food and cargo aboard was a young goat. Someone suggested that this goat be roasted and hung up on the ship's side. Its tempting smell would attract some large sea animal which would fall upon the goat and pull at it and, in so doing, it would tug the ship off the reef. The idea was unanimously accepted; and the young goat was slaughtered and its carcass hung up in the wind. A huge beast drew up to the ship. It fell upon the goat and pulled and pulled. Finally, the ship gave a shudder and slipped back into the water. The sailors cast loose the rope and the beast made off with the goat.

"We are saved! G-d be praised; we are saved!" the people cried and danced on deck in joy. The sailors set course and soon, the ship was on its way. Before long, it had reached its destination — Rome.

R' Eliezer and R' Yehoshua were then visiting Rome when the ship docked. The people aboard told these Jewish Sages about the miracle that had occurred at sea.

They said, "This bears out what King Shlomo said:

'Cast your bread upon the waters...' You were all saved because of the worthy gesture that you made in deciding to divide up all the food equally."

(Adapted from *Midrash Koheles Rabbah 11*)

The Blinding Light

כִּי לֹא יִרְאַנִי הָאָדָם וָחָי

For man cannot see Me and live (33:20)

Hadrian, the Roman emperor, often argued with R' Yehoshua ben Chananya about serious religious matters.

The emperor once asked, "Tell me, is there a Creator? Does someone really rule this world?"

"Certainly!" said R' Yehoshua. "There is a G-d Who guides the world. Could you imagine a world as complex as ours operating by itself?"

"Who created the world?"

"*Hashem*, the A-mighty! Our Torah says so right at the beginning!"

Now came the point of the entire discussion. The emperor said, "If, as you say, there is a G-d, why does He not make Himself visible to the world once in a while. Once or twice a year, for example. Then, all would know that He exists and no one would be able to deny it. And all would then fear Him."

"But that is impossible!" R' Yehoshua explained. "We on earth would not be able to bear the dazzling brilliance of such a sight! Our Torah says, 'For man cannot see Me and live.' "

This is the answer that the emperor had been waiting for. He raised his voice and demanded, "Well, I want to see Him! I, for one, don't believe you. I, Hadrian, Emperor of Rome, demand to see this G-d!"

"But you cannot," R' Yehoshua replied quietly.

Hadrian would not be dissuaded. "I demand that you show Him to me! If you refuse it is a sign that you are lying, that He does not exist!"

R' Yehoshua bowed his head and said, "Very well. Wait until tomorrow."

He left the palace. All that day the emperor could not help thinking about what R' Yehoshua had in mind. How would he show him an invisible G-d, so as not to be proven a liar? He arose early the next morning and waited impatiently for the Sage's arrival.

R' Yehoshua came exactly at noon. He respectfully asked the emperor to step outside with him to the balcony. It was the middle of the summer in the month of *Tammuz,* and the sun was blazing in all its fury. R' Yehoshua lifted his arm and pointed upward, "Look directly into the sun, Your Majesty."

The emperor gasped, "But that is impossible! It is blinding! Who can look straight into the midday sun?!"

R' Yehoshua nodded. "Why does the emperor not listen to his very words! The sun is only one of the myriad servants of *Hashem,* only one of trillions of stars, and you cannot bear to look it in the face. How can you possibly expect to gaze at His blinding glory which fills the entire universe?"

(According to Tractate *Chulin 59b; Yalkut Shimoni I 396*)

Where is the Soul?

כִּי לֹא יִרְאַנִי הָאָדָם וָחָי

For man cannot see Me and live (33:20)

"Tell me, Rabban Gamliel," a gentile once asked, "where is your G-d found? Where is He?"

"I do not know," Rabban Gamliel replied.

"But," said the gentile mockingly, "you Jews pray to Him morning and evening, day in day out. Don't you even know where He is?!"

"What is so unusual?" said Rabban Gamliel. "You possess something that is with you day and night, yet, you do not know exactly where it is located."

"That is impossible!" he retorted, with certainty.

"Yes, indeed. It is your soul. It is always with you. Tell me, if you can, where is your soul located?"

"I don't know," the gentile admitted in confusion.

Rabban Gamliel then said tellingly, "If you cannot tell me where to find something that is present with you all the time, how can you expect me to tell you where *Hashem* is?"

The gentile had been bested this time but nevertheless tried to tease Rabban Gamliel upon another occasion. "Does it not make much more sense," he said," to worship some object that you can see, as we do, rather than to pray to something invisible?"

Rabban Gamliel replied, "You worship something that you can see, but that cannot see you. With us the reverse is true. We worship *Hashem*; He created us and can see us. We, His creations, however, cannot see Him, as it says, 'For man cannot see Me and live."

The Peasant and Shabbos

בֶּחָרִישׁ וּבַקָּצִיר תִּשְׁבֹּת

In the plowing season and in the harvest shall you rest (34:21)

A simple man once came to the court of R' Chaim of Chernowitz, author of *Beer Mayim Chayim*, and wished to receive the Rebbe's holy blessing.

Before he blessed him, the Rebbe asked, "Tell me, do you keep the *Shabbos* properly?"

The man bowed his head in shame and did not reply.

"Do know the importance of the *Shabbos*? Its great sanctity?" he asked. "What possible spiritual pleasure can a farmer like you have all week? You work with the horses and the cows. You are up at dawn, always busy, always under the pressure of your many farm duties. On *Shabbos*, though, a person receives another soul, a cleansed, purified soul. Can there be a greater pleasure than the spiritual one of resting on *Shabbos* and casting aside all the worries and cares of the week? On the other hand, if a person does not have *Shabbos*, what does he have? Unrelenting, constant work, at home and in the fields."

R' Chaim continued, "Our Sages in Tractate *Shabbos* (118b) said: 'If all of Israel would observe only two *Shabbos* days, they would be immediately redeemed from exile!' And does it not appeal to you to become a king? On *Shabbos* one becomes a king in his home. He is free from his weekly worries and reigns supreme!"

These words penetrated deeply into the farmer's heart and he burst into tears. "You are so right, Rebbe. I agree with you. But do you know why I do not observe the

Shabbos, as I should? It is because I rent my farm from the local landlord. I must earn enough for both of us. But now that I have heard what you said, I promise to keep the *Shabbos* in every detail, except, that is... except for harvest time..."

"Why?!" the Rebbe asked, shocked and surprised.

"Because, then I am so overwhelmed with work, that I cannot possibly stop to rest. The harvest work cannot be postponed."

A smile spread over the Rebbe's face. He said, "Let me tell you a true story:

A local landlord, a nobleman, once invited his friends to a gala party. All the gentry from miles around came to feast themselves at his table. When their spirits were high with wine, they began boasting about their Jewish tenants and the loyalty these bore to them. "There is no one like my Jewish tenant," said one. "He would do anything I asked! Anything in the world!" The voice of the host rose above the others and he said, "Perhaps, my friends, but my Jewish tenant is better than any of yours! He is as loyal as a faithful dog and obeys every word I say. In fact, if I told him to convert right now, I am certain that he would do so without any questions!"

"We don't believe you!" the voices hummed all around him. "Idle boasting! Empty talk!"

"You think that I am exaggerating? Very well, I will summon him right now and you will see!" he said, drunkenly.

Soon the Jewish tenant was standing, shaking, before the *poritz.* "Can I trust you to obey everything that I ask of you?" the landlord said.

"Of course! Certainly. Just say the word!" the Jew said ingratiatingly.

"Well then," said the landlord, "I want you to convert to Christianity."

The Jew was taken by surprise. He had not expected such an extreme request! Still, he knew that if he did not give in to the *poritz,* he would be turned out of his home and would be left without any means of livelihood. He nodded his agreement. The landlord sent a servant to fetch the priest and, before long, the Jew was baptized and coverted to Christianity.

A few days passed and the *poritz* came to himself. He suddenly realized what he had demanded from his trusted tenant and was shocked at himself. How could he have done such a terrible thing? He summoned the Jew and apologized, "I am terribly sorry for having caused you such trouble and suffering. It happened in a drunken fit, you understand. But, now, that I am sober and have come to my senses, I am shocked at what I did. Let me assure you, you may return to the religion of your fathers. You may, once again, become a Jew!'

To the landlord's great surprise, the Jew was not too eager. "Thank you for your kind offer, my lord," he said, "but I have been thinking things over. A Jewish holiday is in the offing, the Festival of Passover. As you may know, this is a very expensive holiday. I was wondering if you would not mind if I did not change my religion back for a while, at least until Passover is over."

"What do you think of that little tale?" the Rebbe asked, looking directly at the farmer. "Let me point out another thing. The Torah states: 'Six days shall you work and on the seventh shall you rest. In the plowing time and harvest time shall you rest' (*Shemos* 34:21). This seems somewhat surprising, extra. If the Torah tells us that one must keep the *Shabbos* week in and week out, why does it also specify the plowing and harvest seasons?

"The answer is that even then, when the farmer is besieged with work that cannot be postponed — even then, he must rest and refrain from all work."

"Alas!" moaned the farmer. "How will I manage? Each year my landlord increases my rent. My situation is difficult enough as it is. How will I be able to meet the payments if I do not work every single minute? If I am lax during the harvest and the plowing, I will never get my work done and everything will go to ruin. I will have to resort to begging to keep my family alive!"

R' Chaim had a ready answer, "Our Sages taught that the Torah specifically gave the laws of *Shabbos* to the Jewish people at Mara, the place where the waters were bitter. This is to show us that even when life seems particularly bitter and keeping *Shabbos* seems impossible, a Jew must have faith and keep it anyway. His help will come from *Hashem*, he may be sure of that!"

The Guardian Angels

וְלֹא יַחְמֹד אִישׁ אֶת אַרְצְךָ בַּעֲלֹתְךָ לֵרָאוֹת אֶת פְּנֵי ה׳

No man shall covet your land when you go up to appear before Hashem (34:24)

Our Sages learned from here that those who are sent to perform mitzvos are not harmed.

(Tractate Pesachim 8)

There were once two brothers who lived in Ashkelon. They were pious and industrious and succeeded in business until they became wealthy.

Many begrudged them their success, two gentile neighbors in particular. They envied the Jews' money and constantly plotted against them.

Their chance came. They learned that the brothers were planning to go to Jerusalem for a festival. They would be away for about a week. This would give the wicked neighbors ample time to break into the house and steal whatever they desired.

On the scheduled day, the two brothers arose early, loaded up their donkeys and left. Their gentile neighbors were still sleeping soundly when they went.

When the gentiles awoke, they rushed to their windows to see if the Jews had already left. This was the day that they had been waiting for! They looked towards the Jews' house but to their surprise, saw two figures entering. This was the time that the brothers usually returned from their morning prayers. "Strange," they thought. "But perhaps they will be leaving soon." They waited patiently.

They saw the two brothers leaving the house some time later. But instead of loading up their donkeys for a trip, they went to fetch their farming tools and proceeded out to the fields. Perhaps they intended to go after lunch so that they could arrive in Jerusalem with the evening breeze.

But no. The brothers returned at lunchtime and remained for a short nap. Then they went back to the fields.

The neighbors could not understand it. On the following day, the pattern was repeated. The gentiles were puzzled more than ever and finally had to admit to themselves that the brothers had changed their plans;

they were not going to Jerusalem after all. "Perhaps they found out about our intentions and decided to remain home?" they said to one another.

But, the two brothers had left and were spending the festival in Jerusalem, as planned.

In time, the brothers returned. They had decided to bring some gifts for their friends and neighbors. "Surely they must have kept an eye on our property to see that everything was in order," the brothers thought. "It would be only decent to bring them back some small souvenir from the capital."

They returned late one afternoon and stayed home to rest up. The next morning, however, they paid a visit to the gentile neighbors and gave them the gifts they had brought.

It is difficult to say who was more surprised — the neighbors by the gifts or the brothers by the looks on their neighbors' faces. It took a while to straighten things out.

"Why are you bringing us gifts? You did not go away!"

"What do you mean, we did not go away? Of course we did! Didn't we tell you that we were going to Jerusalem? Why should we not have gone?!"

"But we saw you going in and out of the house, as usual. It was you two. There was no mistake!"

"How can that be? We were away."

The gentiles realized that *Hashem* must have sent angels who looked like the brothers to protect their property. They hung their heads in shame at their evil thoughts. What wonderful people these were. Not only had the brothers not suspected them of any evil, they had been considerate and thoughtful enough to bring back gifts!

"Blessed is the G-d of the Jews Who does not abandon His righteous ones nor will He ever!" they declared enthusiastically.

(According to *Yerushalmi, Pe'ah; Shir HaShirim Rabbah* 7)

R' Zusha's Hashavas Avedah

וַיִּתֵּן עַל פָּנָיו מַסְוֶה

And he put a veil upon his face (34:33)

R' Zusha of Anipoli was very poor. When the time came to marry off his children, he did not have the necessary funds. At the time, R' Zusha was staying with his teacher, R' Dov Ber, the Maggid of Mezeritch. When the Maggid heard about R' Zusha's difficulties, he pressed him to take three hundred rubles, a most sizeable sum in those days.

R' Zusha, at first, refused to accept the money but when the Rebbe insisted, he had no choice; he did not wish to be guilty of disobedience to his master teacher. Feeling very ill at ease, R' Zusha took the large sum and left Mezeritch.

It was a long way to Anipoli. R' Zusha had to travel through many small towns and villages. Along the way he was stopped by the sound of heartbroken sobbing. It came from a tiny hut in a Jewish village. "Who is crying so bitterly?" he asked.

"Oh, yes," he was told. "a poor widow, who was about to marry off her daughter, lives in that hut. On her way to the wedding, she lost the three hundred rubles which was to be her daughter's dowry and the *chasan* refuses to go on with the wedding. Where shall the poor widow find another three hundred rubles? The marriage is off and the mother and daughter are inside weeping."

"Oh, my!" exclaimed R' Zusha. "That is the exact sum I found on my way here." He knocked at the door of the widow's hut, entered and said, "I believe I have found your money, good woman. But tell me first, did it have any marks of identification?"

The widow's eyes lit up with hope. "The money was in nine bills: five of twenty ruble each and four bills of fifty each. Three hundred altogether. They were tied together in a single packet with a plain string."

"Then that is exactly what I found! Rest assured. I will go and fetch it at once." he said, and ran to the local inn where he was staying.

He had the innkeeper change his money into the bills described by the widow and tied them together with a string. He did not want the widow to suspect that the money was not hers.

Meanwhile the good news had spread. Relatives and friends had come rushing and filled the hut, bustling around the *kallah*. By the time Reb Zusha had returned, the band was already playing.

R' Zusha made his way through the crowd. As soon as the people saw who it was, they cleared a path for him, whispering behind his back that this stranger was the man who had found the money and was making the wedding possible after all. They would have lifted him up on their shoulders for joy, but he went straight to the widow and said, "Here is your money. But I am keeping one twenty ruble note for my services." He handed her the bundle of eight notes. Two hundred and eighty rubles in all.

The music stopped and a hush fell on the crowd. People strained to hear what was happening. It was not at all the happy ending they had expected. This was a strange, cruel twist.

"How can you do this?" the widow whispered, shocked. "How can you take a widow's money? You have just fulfilled such a great *mitzvah*! But by taking your reward now, in this world, you will be forfeiting it in the World-to-Come! Why would you want to do such a thing? To sell your reward for a few rubles?"

But R' Zusha held on tightly to the bill. "This money is mine. I demand it for my service."

People began whispering all around them. Everyone was just as shocked as the widow. How could he do such a thing! On the eve of the wedding?

The widow began weeping, "Where do you think I will find another twenty rubles?" Relatives now stepped forward to take her part. They urged R' Zusha to give the widow back her money. They began shouting all kinds of names, "Blackmailer!" "Extortioner!" "Thief! Nothing but a common thief!"

But R' Zusha was unmoved. He held on tightly to his twenty ruble bill.

"We must settle this matter properly," said the family. "You must come with us to the rabbi." They dragged R' Zusha to the local rabbi.

The rabbi listened carefully to the embittered story of the relatives. Then he ruled, "R' Zusha must give back the twenty rubles to the widow!"

The relatives smiled in deep satisfaction. But to their great astonishment, R' Zusha still refused to give back the bill! They pounced upon him and would have torn him limb from limb. But luckily, they found the twenty ruble bill in his pocket. They retrieved it and chased R' Zusha out of town in disgrace.

R' Zusha left and continued on his way. Some time later, after this incident, the rabbi of the village happened to meet the Maggid of Mezeritch.

"Do you know what disgraceful behavior your *talmid* displayed not long ago?" he asked. "R' Zusha came to our town and had the nerve to rob a poor widow on the day of her daughter's wedding!"

The Maggid looked at him severely and said, "As rabbi of the town, it is your duty to go to R' Zusha and beg his forgiveness for the shameful behavior of your townspeople. They were certain that the money he gave to the widow was her lost money. But it was not! It was money that I myself had given him to marry off his own child. As for the twenty rubles which he insisted on keeping, that was not because he wanted the money for himself. He demanded that one bill because he did not want to be honored and thanked for having found and returned the money. He wanted no appreciation for having fulfilled a *mitzvah*. Now you know who R' Zusha is!" the Maggid concluded.

The rabbi set off at once for Anipoli where he found the humble R' Zusha. He begged for forgiveness. R' Zusha reassured him,

"I was never angry with you in the first place. I never resented your ruling that I return the money. As for my honor, I am willing to forgive you, but on one condition only — that you never breathe a word of this story to the widow. I don't want her ever to learn that the money I gave her was not her own!"

All At Once

הַיּוֹם יִוָּדַע כִּי אַתָּה אֶ־לֹקִים בְּיִשְׂרָאֵל

Today it shall be known in Israel that You are Elokim
(Haftorah Parashas Ki Sisa, Melachim I 18)

This story took place at the time of the Spanish Inquisition, when the Church forced all Jews to leave the country or convert. Many Jews chose to remain in Spain and convert publicly but in private, hidden rooms of their home they upheld and practiced all the *mitzvos* of the Torah. If they were caught they were often burned at the stake. These secret Jews were known as Marranos.

Many succeeded in hiding their Jewish identity for years. They even attained high positions in the government. It once happened that a minister was discovered to be practicing Jewish laws in secret. The Inquisition arrested him and put him on trial. He was convicted and was condemned to be burned.

Since this minister was such a capable man, the king intervened and begged the Church to postpone his public execution. He knew that he could not ask for an outright acquittal, for the Church was far too powerful. Once they had a victim in their clutches, they would not let him go. But he was successful in his plea to delay the sentence for one year.

The year was soon up. The Church was eager to make the public display, but the king begged for another reprieve. This time he could ask for no more than a month. This was granted. After that the Jew was granted one more week of life. His public execution was scheduled for the following week.

The king knew that he had done all in his power. Now his trusted, capable minister must die. On the eve of the execution town criers circulated through the city to announce the coming spectacle and urge people to participate. This was to put the fear of the Church into the hearts of all possible heretics.

For many, a public execution was an occasion. The next day people flocked to get a good position so that they could see the great bonfire. Hours before the execution, the town square was already packed. People pushed and shoved forward in order to see.

The condemned man was about to be led to the platform and tied to a wooden post.

Suddenly, without warning, there was a tremor. The ground began shaking and quaking. The people fled in panic, trampling one another in their fear and haste.

The minister seized the opportunity and escaped. He found his way to the palace where the king, his good friend, made arrangements for him to be smuggled out of the country. He crossed the border successfully to freedom.

The former minister wondered about the earthquake which had saved him. Had it been a miracle, or a chance occurrence?

It was very important for him to find an answer. For if it had been a miracle, he felt that he should embrace Judaism with all his heart and openly become a practicing Jew!

He made extensive investigations, reading and asking many questions, trying to determine if that earthquake had been predicted or had come suddenly and unexpectedly. He sought the advice of many wise men, not revealing that he was the man who had been saved by that strange earthquake. Everyone listened to his tale and offered an opinion. The minister was not satisfied; he was still ill at ease.

Finally he heard about one particular rabbi who was reputed to have divine intuition. He traveled to him and arranged to meet him. As soon as he stepped into the rabbi's study, the latter said, "Welcome, eminent minister of Spain!" And the minister had not said a word as yet. He understood that he was in the presence of a holy man.

The rabbi did not even let him speak but said, "As to your question: know that that earthquake had been destined and decreed from the very beginning of Creation. The exact time and place had been planned in advance. But, nevertheless, it was a miracle. For your execution was postponed and postponed. Finally it was rescheduled for the precise moment when the earthquake would occur. Not before or after!"

The minister felt that his question had been answered. He decided on the spot to embrace his fathers' religion openly.

פָּרָשַׁת וַיַּקְהֵל

Parashas Vayakhel

Not the Place for Manners

לֹא תְבַעֲרוּ אֵשׁ בְּכֹל מֹשְׁבֹתֵיכֶם בְּיוֹם הַשַּׁבָּת

You shall not ignite fire in all of your dwellings on the Shabbos day (35:3)

R' Elya Chaim Meisels, rabbi of Lodz, stood guard against the desecration of *Shabbos* in his city.

Once some of his congregants came to R' Elya to inform him that a Jew had been seen lighting a fire in his house. The rabbi immediately put on his hat and coat and marched out.

The suspect saw the rabbi approaching from afar and hastened to put out the fire and destroy any evidence.

R' Elya Chaim arrived at the man's house and barged right in without even knocking first. He wanted to catch the violator redhanded and rebuke him face to face. There was no trace of the fire and the man arrogantly confronted the rabbi with a smug look and said, "A rabbi is supposed to have the minimum of good manners. How come you barged into my house without even knocking?"

R' Elya Chaim replied, "I heard that there was a fire burning in this house. When there's a fire one dispenses with the niceties of good manners and does not wait for permission to enter. One hurries right in to save what one can save."

R' Chanina's Gift

כֹּל נְדִיב לִבּוֹ יְבִיאֶהָ
All the generous of heart shall bring (35:5)

R' Chanina ben Dosa was a great Sage and *tzaddik* who served *Hashem* with all his heart. But he was also very poor.

Once R' Chanina noticed many Jews traveling along the road to Jerusalem. It was right before a Festival, a *yom tov* and they were making a pilgrimage bearing gifts of gold and silver for the *Beis Hamikdash*. They were also leading animals for sacrifices. He looked at their happy faces. How he wished he had something to bring to the *Beis Hamikdash*.

But what could he bring? He could not buy any ornaments of gold or silver. He could not afford an animal for a *korban*. R' Chanina began walking. His feet carried him to the outskirts of the city and the stretches beyond. There, something caught his eye, a beautiful slab of white stone. A stone like this, hewn to a beautiful shape and smoothness would glorify the *Beis Hamikdash*!

R' Chanina began to shape the stone. He worked hard

and long. When he was finished, it was a real work of art. He stood back to admire it and was satisfied with his effort.

He found five strong porters and asked them if they would carry the heavy stone to Jerusalem. They were willing to do so for fifty coins. R' Chainina's heart fell. He only had five.

"Would you be willing to lower your fee to five?" he asked hopefully. They shook their heads and left. R' Chanina was still standing there beside the stone when, suddenly, a group of five men walked by. Where had they come from? He had not even seen them approaching. Hoping against hope, he ventured to ask them if they would be willing to carry his stone to Jerusalem for five coins. They nodded in agreement. They were willing on the condition that he help them. R' Chanina was more than eager to help out!

With a mighty heave the six men lifted the huge mass and began walking. Before R' Chanina even had time to catch his breath they had already reached Jerusalem! The men laid their burden down in the courtyard of the *Beis Hamikdash*. R' Chanina turned to pay them, but they had disappeared. Into thin air! There was no trace of the five men who had carried his heavy stone.

R' Chanina was confused. What should he do now? What should he do about paying the five men? He decided to go to the Sages who sat in the *lishkas hagazis* and tell them the entire story.

When they heard the marvelous tale, they said, "Those men could have been none other than angels sent from Heaven to help you!"

(According to *Koheles Rabbah 1:1*)

The Rejected Donation

כֹּל נְדִיב לִבּוֹ יְבִיאֶהָ אֵת תְּרוּמַת ה׳
All the generous of heart shall bring it (35:5)

Once, R' Yom Tov Algazi was appointed to travel to the Jewish communities in Europe to raise money for the poor of Jerusalem. Wherever he went, he first paid his respects to the rabbi of the city, who would then send his *shammash* out through the streets to inform the people that a visiting scholar from *Eretz Yisrael* would be speaking in the central synagogue. The synagogue would always be packed. When R' Yom Tov would finish speaking and the time came to give, they would open their purses, proud to have a share in the Torah studied in the Holy Land.

In the course of his travels, R' Yom Tov came to the illustrious community of Frankfurt in Germany. This community boasted great Torah giants, among them the rabbi of the community, R' Pinchas Horowitz, the *Ba'al HaHafla'a,* R' Nosson Adler — the Great Eagle — and his young disciple, Moshe Sofer who would go on to become the *Chasam Sofer.*

R' Pinchas Horowitz had the townspeople summoned to the Great Synagogue. R' Yom Tov did not disappoint his audience. When he was finished speaking and asked humbly for support, they gave lavishly and eagerly. People emptied out their wallets and pockets, showering him with money. Among them was one distinguished-looking businessman who approached the rabbi and handed him a bag of gold coins — the largest single sum given.

R' Yom Tov Algazi gathered all of the donations together and warmly thanked his audience for their generous response. He stayed on another day to continue paying his respects to the *gedolim* in the city and exchange *divrei Torah* with them. Then it was time for him to go.

All of the prominent people were there to see R' Yom Tov off, among them the future *Chasam Sofer*. He accompanied the great man for a long way, unable to tear himself away from the mouth that gave forth such gems of wisdom. When he did turn to go, the visitor held R' Moshe back for a minute.

"Here, take this bag of gold coins," he said, handing him the contribution which the distinguished businessman had given him. "I cannot accept it. Return it to the man who gave it. I have a feeling that it is not honestly-gained money."

It was a huge sum. But R' Moshe did not say a word. He took it and returned it to the donor.

A few days later R' Moshe's unasked questions were answered. He learned about the source of the man's wealth: He was a moneylender! He lent money with interest. He had gotten rich on the interest which he had squeezed from his impoverished fellow Jews!

Now R' Moshe understood! "R' Yom Tov was right in rejecting this money as coming from an impure source. He intuitively felt that there was something wrong with the money. "What a great man he was, to have sensed this."

The Chase After the Ring

וְהַנְּשִׂאִם הֵבִיאוּ אֵת אַבְנֵי הַשֹּׁהַם

And the princes brought the onyx stones (35:27)

R' Shmelke of Nikolsburg was famous not only for his vast Torah knowledge and for his piety, but also for his generous heart. He gave charity lavishly and was never known to turn anyone away.

With a reputation like that, he was besieged by the poor all the time, day and night. People came begging for help and no one left emptyhanded.

Once a poor man entered, begging for help. R' Shmelke searched in all of his drawers but could not even find one penny. What could he do? He certainly was not going send him away emptyhanded!

R' Shmelke got up and went into the next room. There, on the table, he spied the *rebbetzin*'s gold ring. He snatched it up and ran into the other room where the poor man was still waiting for him.

"Here," he said. "Take this ring and sell it. The money you get should last you and your family for a long time."

The poor man left the house with a light heart. Just as he had shut the door behind him, the *rebbetzin* came into the room, wringing her hands with distress.

She had lost her ring! She had taken it off to do some work and she was certain that she had left it on the table. But it had disappeared. Where could it be?

R' Shmelke explained that he had given it away to a poor man.

"What?! My diamond ring?! It is worth a fortune! Do you realize what you did?"

She was beside herself. While she was weeping and ranting, the rabbi beckoned to the *shammash* and said, "Run and catch that poor man and tell him..." The rest was a whisper. Off went the *shammash*.

Some time later he returned, puffing and panting but with a smile of victory on his face. "I found him!" he announced joyfully.

The *rebbetzin* expected him to place her ring on the table. But the *shammash* did not have anything for her.

"Where is my ring?" she demanded.

"I was not told to fetch the ring," he explained. She raised her eyebrows questioningly. He continued, "The Rebbe instructed me to find the poor man and inform him that there was a precious stone in the ring he had just received and it was worth a great deal. He was to take care and not let anyone cheat him out of its full value!"

A Gift is a Gift

כָּל אִישׁ וְאִשָּׁה אֲשֶׁר נָדַב לִבָּם אֹתָם

Each man and woman whose heart stirred him (35:29)

There was never any extra money around in the household of R' Zusha of Anipoli. If someone in the family got a new article of clothing, it was cause for celebration. They usually made do with the things they had, mending them over and over to make them serve for another year, another child.

Therefore, when the *rebbetzin* once received a piece of fine cloth, she was overjoyed. This meant a new dress. It was years and years since she had had a new dress. How she looked forward to wearing it. She went to the village tailor and described what she wanted.

He promised that the garment would be ready in a week. Eagerly, a week later, the *rebbetzin* went to pick it up. It was like a *yom tov* for her. When she arrived at the tailor's house, she was in high spirits. But, the good woman could not help noticing tears in the tailor's eyes.

"What is the matter?" she cried out in alarm.

Reluctantly, he poured out his bitter tale. "My daughter recently became engaged. Just this week the *chasan*'s family came to visit and saw the half-finished dress on my table. They remarked over the beautiful material and the fine cut, thinking that this was to be for my daughter. Alas! I am a poor man. I cannot afford to buy material for a new dress for her. Somehow, the family learned that my daughter would not be getting any new clothes. They became very upset and disturbed. I am afraid that this will threaten the very *shidduch*." He choked up and could not talk any more.

The *rebbetzin* thought for a moment, then suddenly picked up the beautiful dress, which had turned out to be a masterpiece, and handed it to the tailor.

"Here! Take this for your daughter! She needs it more than I do." Without waiting for any thanks, she walked out of the house and went home. Her family was waiting for her. The children were looking forward to see their mother bedecked in a new dress. But she returned emptyhanded.

"Where is the dress?" everyone asked.

She told them the entire story and how she had felt that the tailor's young daughter needed it much more than she. R' Zusha listened, then said, "Very nice. But what about the fee? You forgot to pay the tailor for his work!"

The *rebbetzin* was shocked. "What do you mean? I gave him the dress! Why must I pay him for sewing a dress which I will never even wear?"

"But he is a poor man, as you know. He put all of his heart into sewing this dress, expecting to be paid for his work. Do you think that he would have worked so hard for his own daughter? He could not have afforded the time. Laboring over this dress, all week long, he expected to be paid. This money was meant to feed his family. And now you deny him his fee? That is not right! He needs the money for his daily expenses. It was a worthy gesture to give him the dress, but it is not enough. You must pay him for his labor too. Why should he suffer because you want to be generous and give his daughter a gift?"

The *rebbetzin* nodded in understanding. R' Zusha was perfectly right. A gift was one thing and a fee was another.

She rushed right off to pay the tailor for his labor.

The Poor Man's Sacrifice

הוּא וְאָהֳלִיאָב בֶּן־אֲחִיסָמָךְ לְמַטֵּה דָן

He and Oholiav the son of Achisamach of the tribe of Dan (35:34)

Oholiav was from the tribe of Dan, the least of all the tribes, from the sons of the maidservants, the shifchah. And yet Hashem puts him on the same level as Bezalel who was from the most important of tribes, Yehudah! This bears out the verse: "And the nobleman cannot be distinguished from the pauper." (Iyov 34)

(Rashi)

Once King Agrippas wished to donate one thousand animals as sacrifices for the *Beis Hamikdash*. How much glory this would give to his name! He wanted an entire day to be devoted to his sacrifices only and so he sent a message to the *Kohen Gadol*, instructing him not to accept any other sacrifices that day.

On that very day, a poor man came to the *Beis Hamikdash* with his humble offering — two doves. He begged the *kohen* on duty to accept them and sacrifice them.

"But the king gave special instructions that no one was to bring anything today. Can't you postpone it for tomorrow?"

The poor man shook his head sadly and said, "Each day I hunt four pigeons. I bring two of them straight to the *Beis Hamikdash* and the other two I keep for myself. If I do not bring my offering today, I am afraid that I will be endangering my livelihood."

The *kohen* listened to these sincere words and decided to sacrifice the poor man's doves after all, despite the king's orders.

That night the king had a dream. It was revealed to him that some poor man had brought a sacrifice, despite the strict royal orders. When the king awoke, he summoned the *kohen* and said, "Did I not warn you yesterday not to accept any sacrifices other than mine?"

The *kohen* explained, "Yes, Your Majesty. But a poor man came to the *Beis Hamikdash* yesterday with two pigeons. I told him that you had forbade us from accepting anyone's offering, but he insisted that his livelihood depended on it. If he did not bring the two pigeons that day, he would not have food for the morrow. I did not have the heart to refuse him for his life depended on it. And so I accepted his offering, despite my instructions."

The king listened gravely and said, "You did the right thing after all!"

(Midrash Vayikra Rabbah 3:5)

Two Misers

וְהֵם הֵבִיאוּ אֵלָיו עוֹד נְדָבָה בַּבֹּקֶר בַּבֹּקֶר

And they brought more contributions to him morning after morning (36:3)

They brought their donations early, while people were still sleeping, lest their gifts became known.

(Holy writings)

He was known as the Miser of Horodna. Everyone knew that he never gave a penny to charity, that it was a waste of one's time to even approach him.

Nevertheless, R' Nachum once decided to pay the man a visit and ask him for a donation.

He knocked at the door and was ushered in. He remained in the rich man's house for a while and left — with empty hands. People shook their heads, wondering why the Rebbe had bothered altogether. To be sure, he never returned again!

Time went by and the miser passed away. This was the event that many people had been waiting for. Now the townspeople could get back at him and have their sweet revenge for his stinginess throughout the years. The members of the *chevrah kadishah* refused to bury the miser in a prominent place, as befit his wealth. They wished to bury him in a neglected corner by the fence.

When R' Nachum learned of this, he came to the officers of the *chevrah kadishah* with a strange plea. He wanted them to bury the miser in the middle of the cemetery, alongside other distinguished deceased members of the community.

"But he was a terrible miser! He never gave a penny to any charitable or worthy communal cause! Why does he deserve such honor?" they protested.

"His death is his atonement," R' Nachum said. The *chevrah kadishah* could not refuse the rabbi and gave in.

The miser's son continued in his father's footsteps. He was no more generous than his father had been. Not a penny left his clenched fist. The people of Horodna noticed that the rabbi kept away from his home. People assumed that the dead miser, his father, had offended R' Nachum and that was why the Rebbe avoided the son.

Years later, the son passed away too. This time R' Nachum rushed to the *chevrah kadishah,* begging them to bury him in a distinguished plot as well, next to his father. They had no choice but to comply.

More years passed. Now, it was R' Nachum's turn to leave this world. Upon his death, the townspeople opened up their rabbi's will and read the following request: If there is any room beside the grave of the miser and his son, I wish to be buried there.

The townspeople were shocked, but the rabbi left an explanation. When he had entered the miser's home the very first time to request a donation, the latter had explained that he only gave donations in secrecy, *matan beseser*. If R' Nachum guaranteed that he would not tell anyone, the 'miser' was willing to give him a sizeable weekly sum to be distributed among the poor.

And indeed, from that day on, for years and years to come, the rich man had been meeting R' Nachum in some secret place, in the middle of the night, and giving him a large sum of money. His son had continued this same practice after him.

"Should I not desire to be buried next to two such great *tzaddikim*?" R' Nachum's question seemed to hover in the air of Horodna.

Two Bronze Doors

לְדַלְתֵי הַבַּיִת לַהֵיכָל זָהָב

Gold for the doors of the heichal

(Haftorah Parashas Vayakhel, Melachim I 7:3)

And what shall my present to the *Beis Hamikdash* be?" Nikanor asked himself. He decided to contribute two bronze doors.

He was told that the finest bronze and the most talented bronze workers were to be found in Alexandria in the land of Egypt. And so Nikanor sailed to Alexandria to produce his doors.

At last, they were ready; they were beautiful. He had only to transport them to the *Beis Hamikdash*. Nikanor and his doors went aboard ship.

The sailing was smooth at first. The skies were blue and the sea was calm. But a storm suddenly arose. The craft was tossed about. Waves washed aboard. Slowly, the ship began to sink.

The sailors worked desperately to bail out the water but to no avail. The captain came to Nikanor and said, "We must throw one of your bronze gates overboard. It is weighing the ship down and I fear that it will take us down to the bottom of the sea."

Nikanor protested, but no one listened to him. The sailors heaved one precious gate over the side.

The ship rose for a moment, but then began to sink again. "We will have to throw the other gate overboard as well," the captain declared.

This was too much for Nikanor. He threw himself on his remaining door. He clasped it with all his might and exclaimed, "If you throw this overboard, you must throw me along with it as well!"

With these words the sea was suddenly still. The winds calmed and the huge waves disappeared. There was no need to throw the door into the sea after all.

The ship continued on its way and reached port without further mishap. But, Nikanor was heartbroken. True, his life had been saved and one precious door had also been spared. But, one had been lost at sea.

It was now a beautiful day. The sun was sparkling on

the sea and the sea returned its greetings with a merry, twinkling reflection. Nikanor looked listlessly on the pleasant scene. And then, his eye suddenly noticed a large object bobbing up and down in the water. It caught the gleaming sunlight and reflected it back with coppery highlights. Nikanor looked hard, not believing his eyes.

It was! It was his lost door, floating behind the ship. It had not sunk. It had followed in the wake of the ship, all the way to the port. What a miracle! Nikanor was beside himself with joy. Here was the match of the door on board. He had the complete pair!

The doors were carried to Jerusalem where they were affixed to one of the gateways leading to the courtyard of the *Beis Hamikdash*. It was henceforth called the Nikanor Gate. Many years later, when all the other doors were replaced or plated with gold, this pair of doors remained in their bronze glory, a testimonial to the marvelous miracle.

(Adapted from Tractate *Yoma 38a*)

פָּרָשַׁת פְּקוּדֵי

Parashas Pekudei

The Child in Prison

הַמִּשְׁכָּן מִשְׁכַּן הָעֵדֻת

The mishkan, mishkan of the testimony (38:21)

Hamishkan mishkan — it is written twice to hint that it was pawned (nismashken) during the two Destructions because of the sins of Israel

(Rashi)

Upon one of his many trips to Rome, R' Yehoshua ben Chananya was once told that a shipload of captives from *Eretz Yisrael* had been brought into the city. One of the prisoners was a young child. They were sure that he was a Jewish child; he had a special air of purity about him. R' Yehoshua went to the prison where the captives were being held. He stood outside not far from the prison. Sure enough, at one of the tiny barred windows was a small figure, looking out, yearning for freedom.

R' Yehoshua began talking aloud, as if to himself. He quoted a verse from *Yeshaya:* "Who has allowed Yaakov to be trampled under and Yisrael to be plundered?"

R' Yehoshua's voice reached the lad. He looked out at the figure down below and completed the verse, "Is it not *Hashem* against Whom we have sinned and Whose ways we refused to follow and Whose Torah we did not obey?"

R' Yehoshua had learned that this was a Jewish youngster. He was also convinced that the lad possessed an exalted soul and that he should be redeemed, at all costs and all effort. He put himself to the task and after much labor succeeded in freeing him.

The boy returned to *Eretz Yisrael* and continued his studies. He learned diligently for many years and became a famous rabbi and teacher.

And who was this wonderful child who was saved from slavery?

Our Sages say that it was R' Yishmael ben Elisha who later became the close friend and learning companion of R' Akiva.

(Adapted from Tractate *Gittin 58a; Eichah Rabbah 4:4*)

The Rebbe Builds

וַיָּקֶם מֹשֶׁה אֶת הַמִּשְׁכָּן
And Moshe erected the Mishkan (40:18)

They were building a new synagogue in Belz. And R' Shalom, the rabbi, was helping with the work.

One day, R' Shalom's older brother, R' Leibush Rokach, came to visit their mother who lived with R' Shalom. He was aghast to find R' Shalom toiling like a common workman — passing bricks and mixing cement, just like one of the construction crew. R' Leibush felt it necessary to rebuke R' Shalom. "It says in the *gemara* that when a person has been appointed community leader, a *parnas*, he is no longer permitted to do any menial work in front of three men or more. You, my dear brother, are the *rav* of Belz, the Admor, why do you disregard this rule?"

R' Shalom listened to his brother's scolding and was silent for a moment. Finally he explained his behavior: "When I was a student in Skohl, I studied Torah together with two very close friends. It was revealed to us that if we diligently labored over our studies for one thousand consecutive nights without sleep, we would be rewarded with a revelation from Eliyahu Hanavi. We yearned for such a holy revelation and devoted ourselves to this holy task. At first we encountered no difficulties. Night after night we pored over the Torah with utter concentration and devotion. But as time went on, the lack of sleep began to tell on us and it became increasingly difficult to stay awake. After several hundred nights of study, one of us faltered and gave up. He could not keep up the pace. My friend and I continued on together, studying intensely night after night until by the eight hundredth night he, too, fell by the wayside, unable to keep up. I remained alone. Being so close to my goal, I resolved that nothing would stop me from completing the one thousand consecutive nights. It was not easy. But the hope of divine revelation made me push on.

"The thousandth night finally arrived. It was stormy. Fierce winds blew and one particularly strong blast burst open the windows of the *beis medrash*, smashing the glass and extinguishing my candles. It was pitch dark; I could no longer learn. The wind blew the rain into the room, blowing terror into my heart. I would have run home, except that I was too afraid of the storm to budge from my spot. I realized well enough, that this was my last night. If I did not complete this thousandth night, I would forfeit all nine hundred and ninety-nine days of effort. Was I to be prevented from achieving my hard-earned reward because of this storm?

"Tears of frustration flowed freely down my cheeks. In my desperation, I got up and groped my way in the dark to the *aron kodesh*. When my hand felt the wooden door, I slid it open and began pouring out my bitterness before *Hashem*. *'Ribono shel olam,'* I cried, 'have pity on me. Do not let all of my efforts go to waste!'

"I wept and pleaded until *Hashem* finally had mercy on me. The storm subsided; all was quiet outside. Suddenly, I heard some footsteps. I looked up and saw an old man enter the *beis medrash*. It was Eliyahu Hanavi. He approached me and we began to learn together. We studied Torah all that night.

"Do you know, dear brother," said R' Shalom, "the last *halachah* that he taught me was one of the laws of the synagogue. And now that we are building a new synagogue here in Belz do you think that I will delegate this holy labor to workmen without lifting a finger myself? If it were in my power, I would build the entire structure from foundation to rafters. But since I do not have the strength or the skill, I try to do the little that I am able. I can think of no greater privilege!"

הַפְטָרוֹת מְיֻחָדוֹת

מָחָר חֹדֶשׁ
שַׁבָּת וְרֹאשׁ־חֹדֶשׁ
אַרְבַּע פָּרָשִׁיּוֹת
שַׁבָּת הַגָּדוֹל

Machar Chodesh
Shabbos Rosh Chodesh
Arba Parashiyos
Shabbos Hagadol

Self-Sacrifice for a Jew

יְהוֹנָתָן וְדָוִד
Yehonassan and David
(Haftorah Machar Chodesh, Shmuel I)

There once lived a Jewish butcher in a port city. He had been poor in his youth, but later became very successful and wealthy for he was capable and efficient. He was not a learned man, having only grasped the elements of reading. But he did know how to pray and say *Tehillim.*

Although he was only a simple Jew, he was a good person at heart and a generous one. In his prosperity he did not forget the lean days, when he had been close to starvation. And so, each *erev Shabbos,* he would distribute meat to all the poor families in the city. He also gave money generously to all who asked.

The butcher became a well known and well liked figure in the city. Even the ruler himself favored him and appointed him as customs officer for all the ships that docked at the harbor. His duties were to inspect every ship that came in and to collect the customs for the merchandise being brought in. Aside from his fee, the butcher was allowed to take any one item that caught his fancy. With a job like this, it was no wonder that he grew wealthier and wealthier.

Once a ship sailed into the harbor and, as usual, the butcher went to inspect its cargo. The captain showed the officer what he was bringing in, merchandise of all kinds, and the butcher charged him accordingly. When he had finished his inspection the captain took him aside and whispered in his ear, "I am also carrying something else but I am not at liberty to reveal what it is. I am willing, however, to sell it to you if you like."

The butcher looked at him in surprise. What was the meaning of such an offer? Whoever bought merchandise sight unseen? How could he know what it was worth and if he wanted it altogether? He was about to turn his back on the captain when his curiosity overcame him. "What is it?" he asked, despite himself.

"Oh, I cannot tell you unless you agree to buy it first. And you must pay for it in advance even before you see it. But it is a one-time chance. If you don't buy it now, I will never offer it to you again!"

The butcher's curiosity grew. What could this mysterious item be? He wanted to buy it, if only to satisfy that curiosity. And so he asked, "How much do you want for it?"

"Ten thousand gold coins!"

"For such a price I deserve at least to see the merchandise, don't you think?"

"I am sorry. You must pay first. Then I will give you the prize."

The butcher could not contain his curiosity by now and wavered. But the wily captain was no longer willing to give him the merchandise for ten thousand gold coins. He now doubled the price. "Twenty thousand! Not a penny less!"

That was a fortune! An enormous sum, even for a wealthy tax collector. What could possibly be worth such a price?

When he saw the man hesitating, the wily captain changed his mind and said, "No! I don't think I will sell it for twenty thousand but for forty. It is worth that much!"

The butcher was almost ill with curiosity by now. It must be a very valuable treasure to fetch such a price. And if he hesitated any longer, the price would soar again. He decided to gamble. "All right, I will pay your price. But first show me what you have."

"No! First you lay out the money. Then I will give you what you bought."

Against his better judgment, the butcher returned home to gather the huge sum together. He came back to the captain some time later with the money. After the entire sum was carefully counted, the captain went down into the hold of the ship to fetch the merchandise.

He returned a few minutes later with a large number of captives in tow. These were Jewish men and women and children. The butcher had bought himself two hundred captives.

The wicked captain smirked at him and said, "Are you not happy? Is this not a bargain even for forty thousand gold coins? Let me tell you now that had you not agreed to pay for these prisoners, I would have thrown them into the sea for I have no use for them."

The butcher left the ship as quickly as he could, taking the prisoners along with him to dry land before the captain changed his mind again.

He took the unfortunate prisoners to his house. There he bathed and treated them, clothed and fed them like a loving father. When they had recovered somewhat from their ordeal, the prisoners told him how these pirates had come to their village and seized them by force, destroying their houses and taking them into captivity. They had starved in the bowels of the ship for weeks, for no one had wanted to buy them.

The butcher saw to it that the people found jobs and homes. There was one young girl among the captives who caught his eye. "She would be fine for my son," he thought. The match was arranged and preparations made for a lavish wedding. Everyone was to be invited to this grand affair, all the poor of the city as well.

The great day finally arrived. The butcher circulated among his guests feeling like a king. How happy he was to receive everyone's good wishes. As he was walking about, he suddenly spied a young man weeping in a corner. He recognized him as one of the men whom he had freed. He hurried over to him and asked, "Why are you crying? You should be happy today. Everyone here is rejoicing with me."

At first the youth remained silent, the tears coursing down his cheeks. But upon the butcher's urging, he admitted the cause of his pain. With a deep gulp, he began his tale,

"The bride who is to be married to your son today was really my betrothed. We were to have been married shortly, but were kidnapped by the pirates. How shall I not weep as I see her being given to another?"

"I did not know anything about this. Why didn't you tell me?" the butcher said, aghast.

"How could I say anything, after all you did for us, for

the entire village?"

The butcher was pensive. Finally he got up. He had made his decision. He went over to his son, the *chasan* and took him aside and told him the story. The young man insisted that the prisoner should have the young bride. He did not wish to stand between them and happiness.

The father beamed at his son. He was proud of him. He then went to the bride to inform her of the change in plans. A wedding took place that day as scheduled; the bridegroom was a surprise for the guests.

After the wedding, the butcher continued to take an interest in the couple. He bought them a house, furnished it and gave them a large sum to set themselves up in life.

When the Sages learned of this *chesed* they said that the butcher acquired a great treasure with his forty thousand gold coins, a great *mitzvah* of kindness which has no like! Surely this man deserved an honorable share in the World-to-Come, alongside the great men of his people!

(According to *Yalkut Hasipurim 37* in the name of an early *Tanchuma*)

For What to Be Thankful

וְאֶל זֶה אַבִּיט אֶל עָנִי וּנְכֵה רוּחַ

Upon this will I look, at the poor and the broken in spirit
(Haftorah Shabbos Rosh Chodesh, Yeshayah 67)

The entire city talked about the matter. A match had been arranged between the son and daughter of two wealthy families. But, right after the engagement, the daughter's father had fallen on hard luck and was so impoverished that he could not pay the dowry he had promised for his daughter. The *chasan*'s father threatened to dissolve the engagement unless the *kallah*'s father produced the entire sum. But the poor man did not own a penny to his name!

The desperate father of the girl went so far as to demand that the *chasan*'s father provide the dowry for the couple. It was no wonder that the entire city found no other subject to talk about except the prospective wedding. Would it take place? Who, in the end, would provide the dowry?

Upon the poor man's insistence that the other party pay the dowry, the rich man decided to take the matter to a *din Torah* before the astute R' Chaim of Sanz, rabbi of the nearby town.

The girl's father refused to appear, for he guessed that he would be made to pay up on his promise or dissolve the match. He was unable to do the first and refused to agree to the second.

The angry father of the young man decided to go to Sanz himself and present his case. It was a Friday. By the time he arrived it was already past noon and the Rebbe was making his preparations to usher in the *Shabbos.*

The wealthy man hardly expected a cordial reception at this late hour. But to his great surprise, the Sanzer Rebbe greeted him warmly, asked about his affairs and was even prepared to hear all the complaints he wished to lodge against the co-signer of the engagement contract, the father of the bride.

The father of the young man explained at length exactly what had happened while the Rebbe listened intently. When he finished, the Rebbe rose and began pacing the floor, deeply engrossed in his thoughts. Finally he looked up at the rich man and said, "It is an involved matter which I cannot answer at once. It is Friday afternoon, right before *Shabbos.* I need time to think the matter over. But let me tell you one thing, you should be glad that you came to me..."

These few words put hope into the rich man's heart. His eyes lit up with thanks and appreciation. As he left the room, he thought to himself, "The Rebbe said that I should be thankful that I came to him. Surely, this means that he will find some way to make the girl's father produce the dowry. How truly glad I am that I came here!"

He remained in Sanz that *Shabbos.* After *havdalah* he went into the Rebbe's room, full of confidence that what the Rebbe said now, after having thought it over at length, would be in his favor.

To his astonishment, the Rebbe said, "This match must go through and furthermore, you must provide the bride's dowry. Nor must there be any delay in the wedding or stinting in the expenses thereof!" the Rebbe said emphatically.

The rich man was thunderstuck. Had he heard correctly? His hands began trembling; his heart pounded; blood rushed to his face.

When he recovered somewhat from the shock he dared to ask, "Now that I hear what the Rebbe has ruled, I cannot help expressing my surprise at what the Rebbe said to me on *erev Shabbos*. Why should I have been thankful that I came here? The ruling is not at all favorable to me. Any other rabbi would not have dealt as harshly with me when the claim of the girl's father is not at all justified."

R' Chaim broke out into a smile which confused the rich man even more. Finally, R' Chaim explained himself, "I see that you misunderstood what I said to you on *erev Shabbos*. I said that you should be grateful that *you* came to me! It could have been the other way round, that you had been the rich man who lost all of his property and turned pauper. It could just as easily have been the girl's father who had remained rich and come to me to force you to pay your obligation.

Since it was you, rather than he, who came to me, you have much to be thankful for; you are able to pay for both your side and hers."

The wealthy man now understood the Rebbe and with a joyous heart he returned home to make preparations for the upcoming wedding.

Charity Saves From Death

כֶּסֶף נַפְשׁוֹת עֶרְכּוֹ
The money as each man is rated
(Haftorah Parashas Shekalim, Melachim II 12)

Two learned men once lived in *Eretz Yisrael*: one was a Jewish scholar and the other a gentile astrologer.

Shmuel, the Jew, was once sitting near a lake when his neighbor, Avlet the stargazer, happened to pass and sat down beside him. Large rushes, which people used to cut for basket-weaving, grew by the lake shore.

As they sat there, a group of workers passed by. They were coming to cut down the bulrushes to weave mats and make flutes to sell in the city. As soon as they passed close by, the stargazer pointed to one of the men and whispered in Shmuel's ear, "Do you see that man? I know that he will not come back alive. Misfortune will overtake him."

Shmuel replied, "If that man is a Jew then he will return safely, for I will pray for him, or perhaps he will perform some good deed that will save his life."

The two men sat to await the outcome of their 'contest'. The workers continued on to the lake shore and began cutting down the rushes. It was difficult work for the rushes were high and they had to be bound together in bundles. They worked for many hours before, finally, calling a break to eat and rest. It was customary for these workers to pool together all of their food and then share it equally. They were about to do so when the man whom the stargazer had singled out looked at his companion and noticed how sad he looked. He understood, at once, that he had not had any money to buy food that day and so his satchel was empty. But he was embarrassed to say so to the others.

The man thought quickly. "I do not want my companion to feel bad. I must help him and prevent him from being embarrassed before the others, but I must do so in such a way that it will not be noticed." He took the basket which was used for gathering the food and announced, "Today is my turn to collect the food and distribute it." He went from worker to worker, collecting the food each one had brought. When he reached his neighbor, the man whose satchel was empty, he pretended to take what was inside and put it in the communal basket. Instead, he put in bread that he himself had brought.

When the basket was full and everyone had contributed, he began dividing up the contents equally. Everyone else received a fair share. But he took the smallest portion for himself, though no one noticed anything. Then they all sat back and enjoyed their lunch and rest. His partner, the man who had not brought anything, ate along with the rest without embarrassment.

After the meal, the workers went back to work. Towards evening, each one took the bundle of rushes which he had cut that day and heaved it on to his back.

Walking in single file, they started back towards the city.

Shmuel and Avlet were sitting in the same place. They had returned to see the outcome of their 'contest'. They looked at the line of workers and saw that the same number was returning as had gone. Avlet was furious for this showed his prediction to be false. He jumped up and went over to the worker whose death he had predicted and demanded,

"Show me the bundle of rushes that you cut today."

The man was surprised at his request and his angry tone, but seeing by the stranger's appearance and look that he was a learned man, he swung the bundle of rushes off his shoulder and laid it on the ground.

"Aha!" said the astrologer, pointing to something between the rushes. "That is a poisonous snake. It should have bitten and killed you. You bound it up together with your rushes, crushing it to death."

He turned triumphantly to Shmuel and said, "See! I was right! If the snake had bitten him, he would not have returned alive with the rest! My prediction was correct to begin with. I don't know what happened to make it go wrong. I don't know why this man was saved."

Shmuel now turned to the bewildered worker, "Did you do any worthy deed this day?"

"Yes, I did," he replied, somewhat flustered. He went on to tell how he had cleverly spared his companion embarrassment at not having brought any lunch but had let him share along with the rest.

"You certainly did a worthy deed," exclaimed Shmuel. "a *mitzvah*. You fulfilled the commandment of loving your fellow man like yourself. This good deed saved your life!"

(According to Tractate *Shabbos 156b*)

Deserters Will Be Punished

הַחֵפֶץ לַה׳ בְּעֹלוֹת וּזְבָחִים כִּשְׁמֹעַ בְּקוֹל ה׳

Does Hashem desire burnt offerings and sacrifices as greatly as listening to the voice of Hashem?

(Haftorah Parashas Zachor, Shmuel I 15)

It was the eve of *Yom Kippur* in Brisk. The congregation had already finished saying the *Kol Nidre* and the *maariv* service. Many of the worshippers had already gone home but others remained behind in the synagogue to recite *Tehillim*, as was the custom.

R' Yosef Dov, the *rav* of Brisk, noticed one particular man settling down to say some psalms and went over to him. He was a rich man known for his stinginess. R' Yosef turned to him and said, "When a soldier deserts his unit and runs away from the army he has committed a capital offense. It is treason. But what about a soldier who deserts the infantry and goes over to the artillery without permission? Does he also deserve to be killed for insubordination?"

The wealthy man looked at the Brisker *rav* with utter amazement. What possible connection could such a strange question have with *Yom Kippur*? What did R' Yosef Dov want from him?

The great man continued by answering the question himself, "Yes, indeed. A soldier who deserts his infantry division and goes over to artillery must also face punishment."

The rich man was more confused than ever.

"Let me explain, my friend. We are all soldiers of *Hashem*. We are all charged with duties, each man according to his capabilities and circumstances. Each of us is assigned to his own unit. The rich man must serve *Hashem* on *erev Yom Kippur*. He must return all of the heirlooms, jewelry and other objects given to him as security by poor people who have not been able to get together the money to repay their loans. It is his duty to give out charity and do acts of *chesed* on the day before *Yom Kippur*. The poor man, who cannot be generous with charity, has other tasks; he must do the two other things which also help avert evil and harsh decrees for the coming year — he must pray and repent.

It is customary for the poor to remain behind in synagogue on the night of *Yom Kippur* and recite *Tehillim*, for that is what they are capable of doing. The rich men, who have hopefully already fulfilled their duty to the community by doing acts of charity, can go home to sleep. Each soldier must carry out his orders; after he has done so satisfactorily, he is free to go to sleep. But no soldier is permitted to move from one division to another!

You, my friend, have done exactly that. You have deserted your unit and transferred without permission to another one. You have avoided your obligations as a man in the rich division and sought duties belonging to another unit altogether, that of the sayers of *Tehillim*. Yet you are no less a deserter, no less disloyal. And for that, you deserve to be punished!"

The rich man lowered his eyes in shame. He understood very well what the rabbi had been trying to tell him.

The Miser Turned Beggar

וַהֲסִרֹתִי אֶת־לֵב הָאֶבֶן מִבְּשַׂרְכֶם
I will remove the heart of stone from your flesh
(Haftorah Parashas Parah, Yechezkel 36)

Reuven was a prominent Jew in every respect except one. He was very wealthy and also most learned. His greatest fault, however, was his stinginess. Everyone knew that Reuven never gave a penny away.

It was evening when this story begins:

The evening services were over. Reuven was about to go home when he noticed a stranger remaining behind in the *beis medrash,* taking down a book from one of the shelves and sitting down to pore over it.

This particular man was a wandering beggar who had been on the road for many weeks. He had hardly eaten these last few days and was on the verge of starvation. How pleasantly surprised the stranger was, therefore, when someone tapped him on the shoulder and invited him to his house. "I am sure to get a decent meal there," he thought hopefully, seeing the prosperous look of his host. "He might even ask me to sleep over. Oh for a warm, soft bed! How long it has been since I have slept in a proper bed."

With a light step, the poor man got up and followed behind the man who had invited him. Little did he know that he was going straight to the home of Reuven, the local miser!

Reuven asked the visitor to sit down at the table while he went to wash his hands for supper. He returned, said the blessing over bread, and began to eat heartily. Throughout the meal he turned to his guest and exchanged Torah ideas but not once did he ask him to join him. Reuven seemed to enjoy his guest's company for as he had guessed, the stranger was a learned person who had fallen on hard times. After he had finished and wiped his mouth daintily on his napkin, Reuven thanked his guest for his pleasant company and nodded, signaling for him to leave.

When he left Reuven's house, he was so weak that he did not even have the strength to return to the synagogue. He dropped down on the road and died. Perhaps, if the poor man had remained in the synagogue, he would not have met his end so quickly.

His body was discovered early the next morning. The entire city buzzed with the news; everyone knew that he had last been seen going to Reuven's house. They also knew that he had died of starvation. Apparently, Reuven had not given him even a morsel of bread.

Reuven also realized that the poor man's death was his fault. He regretted his blind stinginess and yearned to cleanse himself from this terrible sin. He decided to travel to a famous *tzaddik* who lived nearby and seek a form of penance. When he arrived at the Rebbe's house, he burst into tears and, sobbing, told his story with bitter remorse. "What can I do to atone for this terrible sin?" he asked.

"Come back tomorrow," the wise man replied. "I will tell you exactly what you must do."

When Reuven returned on the following day, the Rebbe said, "Your sin is truly a very serious one. Heaven has informed me of the only path open to you for repentance but you must follow my instructions to the very letter, no matter how difficult you find it." Reuven nodded wordlessly and the sage went on. "Go to your local *beis medrash* but stop off at your house on your way there. Take your *tallis* and *tefillin* and leave a note that you have been called away suddenly on an urgent business matter which will keep you away for a long time. Afterwards you are to remove your fine clothing and put on beggars' rags. You will be surprised to see that your very face and form will change so that you are unrecognizable. Disguised as a traveling beggar, you are to go directly to the synagogue.

"You are to spend the next year of your life within the walls of this *beis medrash*. You shall devote all of your time to prayer and Torah study though you many lie down on a bench to sleep for a few hours each night. The kind people of this town will certainly offer you meals and perhaps even lodgings but you must refuse every such invitation.

"You will be on the verge of starvation. When you feel that you can no longer bear your hunger, you may leave the synagogue. But the only place where you may seek food is in your own house. You must knock at your door and beg for some food. Of course, your family will not recognize you and having been well trained by your stinginess, will chase you away from the door. You must go back again and again until they give you something to eat, scraps left for the cat or the hens. You will learn to feel exactly what it is to be at the mercy of others, to be starving and to be turned away with ridicule. You will be made to pay for your sins measure for measure!

"Under no circumstances must you reveal your identity

to anyone! Nor must you approach any other house but your own for food. As soon as you receive the scraps of food, you are to eat them quickly and return at once to the synagogue where you must continue to study and pray. This is to be the schedule of your life. This is the only way open to you, so make the best of this chance."

"How long is this penance to last?" Reuven asked.

"For one full year! Twelve whole months! If you can last through the year, you will know that your repentance has been accepted and you can return to normal life. But if you die during this time, your death itself will be atonement."

Reuven did as the *tzaddik* had told him. Dressed in rags, he saw that no one recognized him. He took a place behind the stove where no one would notice and saw the synagogue filling up. His own place, Reuven's seat at the eastern wall, was conspicuously vacant. He half expected someone to nudge him and tell him to go to his seat but realized that this was an idle dream. He had a different role to play now. He was a stranger, a beggar. No one guessed that he was disguised.

People came over to him and put pennies in his hand but he repeatedly refused all donations. At the beginning, people often invited him to their homes for a meal but he declined their offers. In the end, the townspeople left him alone, taking him for a madman.

Three days passed thus. Three days of fasting. By the end of the third day he felt himself about to collapse. The time had come to go and beg for food.

He dragged himself weakly through town to his own house. A maid answered his knock but chased him away at once. He knocked again and again until finally he was rewarded with a dry crust of bread which had been put aside for the chickens. He was also given a glass of water. By soaking the bread in the water he was able to chew and swallow it down.

Reuven returned to his bench in the *beis medrash* and resumed his *teshuvah* through study and prayer. Another three days passed. He went to his house and knocked on the door but received the same harsh treatment as before. After hours of banging away on the door and being rebuffed, the maid finally let him have some dry crusts and a glass of water.

Thus did his days pass. Weeks became months. But it was a very difficult time for poor Reuven. He sometimes thought that he might be better off dying rather than suffer such humiliation at his own home. But hunger always won out in the end and he kept on going back for the dry crusts which barely kept him alive. He spoke to no one during all this time and felt terribly lonely. He longed to be together with his family; he longed for the comfort of a home, a bed, a table and a decent meal. He missed his family too. Sometimes he felt that he could not go on any longer, that if he did not eat he would die. But he survived.

When Reuven recalled what had brought him to such a state, he would feel grateful that at least he was able to atone for his terrible sin during his lifetime. If he survived, he could return to his family, the Rebbe had promised. He had that to look forward to during the dreary days of hunger and discomfort.

All twelve months finally went by. And Reuven was still alive! This meant that his penitence had been accepted. How happy he was!

When the year was over, Reuven left the synagogue in his beggarly garb for the last time and changed back to his fine clothing. He then went home to his family. What rejoicing! His wife and children could hardly recognize him, he had become so thin and his sunken eyes were so filled with a pain behind his apparent joy at seeing them again. But it was their Reuven, no mistake.

"Where were you all this time? Where did you disappear to?" they asked him, full of curiosity at his strange absence.

"We had no word from you for a whole year! Tell us, where have you been and why do you look so thin?" his wife asked, full of concern.

"Let me first rest up. Tomorrow we will hold a feast of celebration and I will tell you everything," he promised.

The news of Reuven's return spread through the town. But even greater was the surprise at his announcement that the entire town was invited to his homecoming feast. This was so out of character! Reuven, who had never invited anyone to his home, had never spent an unnecessary penny. He had also announced that all the poor of the city were expected to come. Stranger than ever! People eagerly awaited the morrow and the unraveling of the strange riddles.

They came the next day to witness the change in Reuven with their own eyes. There he was, thinner than usual, urging them to taste of the bounty laden tables, begging them to eat their fill! It was unbelievable!

Everyone sat down to eat and rejoice with their host. But in the middle of the festivities, when they were waiting for him to rise and explain the mystery that gnawed away at their curiosity, they looked around and saw that Reuven had disappeared. "Where has he gone?"

"Perhaps he has left us again for another year?" some people suggested. "This is getting stranger and stranger!"

They got up to search for their host and suddenly, discovered the mad pauper whom they had not seen for two days. What was he doing here? He never left his place behind the stove in the synagogue.

People began jokingly to offer him food and money, knowing that he would refuse in his strange way, as he always did. They laughed at his expense but he did not seem to mind. He seemed in especially good spirits today, far happier than they had ever seen him.

The beggar walked between the tables of the guests until he came to the head table where the entire family sat. He walked over to Reuven's place, raised both of his hands for silence and then said:

"I would like to have everyone's attention for a few minutes."

All eyes focused on this strange man who had lived in their midst for twelve months but who had never spoken a word to anyone. Now he was facing them all and making a speech! "What does he want?" people whispered to one another. "Is he going to become mad before our eyes?"

"Look at me well, my friends. Can you recognize me? I am Reuven!" His words were greeted by a wild outburst of laughter.

"I really *am* Reuven. Wait, while I go inside to change my clothing and you will see that I am not fooling you. When I return I will clear up the mystery. I will answer all of your questions."

The guests were dumbstruck. They waited in silence for the strange man to return, half believing that he spoke the truth. He returned a few minutes later, dressed in Reuven's clothing, but holding his tattered rags up high for them to see.

"Do you see this suit? This served me faithfully for twelve long months. This is now my greatest treasure. I will guard it jealously and always look at it with the deepest respect for it taught me a most valuable lesson. It was my penance. It taught me how important it is to help others, to be charitable and good, to help those less fortunate. It taught me what suffering is so that I will now be able to sympathize with others in trouble. These rags will always symbolize to me the great mercy of *Hashem* Who enabled me to do *teshuvah* and Who accepted it without taking my life. Today I feel like a newborn man! I have been granted new life. That is the real reason for this celebration."

Reuven finished his brief speech and looked all around him at the people he knew so well. And they looked back at him, hardly believing their eyes. They knew that he was a changed man and marveled. They joined him in thanksgiving at this new chance which he had been given to begin life afresh. They knew that he had learned his lesson well.

It is Cold in His House Too!

וְעָשָׂה הַנָּשִׂיא בַּיּוֹם הַהוּא בַּעֲדוֹ וּבְעַד כָּל עַם הָאָרֶץ

And the prince shall prepare for himself and for all the people of the land

(Haftorah Parashas Hachodesh, Yechezkel 45)

"Do you know that R' Chaim's firewood shed is always open?" one person commented to another.

"Why? Doesn't he have a lock on it?" the other asked.

"No, he doesn't. It is always open. Poor people come and go. They take what they want as if it belonged to them."

This did not please the second man at all. "That is not right. R' Chaim's firewood is paid for by community funds."

Two leaders of the community of Brisk had found out that their rabbi allowed the poor to take freely from his own supply of firewood and they were not pleased.

"No! We will not stand for this!" they decided firmly. "We will lock the storeroom and give the key to R' Chaim!"

Soon a stout lock hung from the door of the shed. The only key was given to the rabbi's loyal *shammash*.

R' Chaim learned of this very soon and demanded that the lock be removed. The shed stood wide open, as before, accessible to all the poor of the city. And once again the poor came and took according to their needs.

When the community leaders came to R' Chaim with their complaint that the community chest could not afford to supply him with limitless firewood, he threw up his hands in despair and said, "I am sorry, gentlemen. If that is the case, then I must forego the privilege of firewood for myself for I cannot possibly sit in a well-heated home knowing that there are poor families in Brisk that are freezing."

What the Mice Had to Say

הָבִיאוּ אֶת כָּל הַמַּעֲשֵׂר... וְגָעַרְתִּי לָכֶם בָּאֹכֵל וְלֹא יַשְׁחִית לָכֶם
אֶת פְּרִי הָאֲדָמָה

Bring all the tithes... and I will rebuke the devourer for your good lest he destroy the fruit of the land
(Haftorah Shabbos Hagadol, Malachi 3)

R' Pinchas ben Yair tried to fulfill one particular *mitzvah* — that of freeing Jewish captives. He used to wander among villages and towns to collect money so that he could redeem prisoners and slaves from their owners.

Once he came to a city, which he visited occasionally, to collect money. The people went out to greet him, as usual, but R' Pinchas noticed that they looked distressed and sad.

"What is the matter?" he asked. "What is troubling you?"

The people sighed and replied, "We are suffering from a terrible plague. We fear that we will all starve, sooner or later."

"Why?!" R' Pinchas asked in amazement. "This past year was blessed with plentiful rains and a rich harvest.

Why should you be afraid of starvation?"

"What you say is true," the townspeople agreed, "but we are unable to enjoy the plentiful harvest. Our fields are infested with mice. They have overrun our barns and are destroying our entire crop. We trap them, but they increase very rapidly and we cannot cope with this terrible plague! We have prayed, Rebbe, but nothing has helped. What should we do?"

R' Pinchas sympathized with the stricken city and promised to do what he could. R' Pinchas was very righteous and *Hashem* gave him the wisdom to understand why the city was afflicted with mice. As soon as he knew the reason, he gathered all of the townspeople to a large open field and standing in the middle of it, commanded all of the mice to appear before him. Although by nature mice are afraid of humans, they obeyed the Sage's command and came by the hundreds and thousands. Within minutes the field swarmed with the tiny creatures. They crowded together, but still took up a lot of room. The air was filled with their shrill chattering and squeaking. The noise grated on the ears of the townspeople and they tried to shut it out by stopping up their ears but the noise grew louder and louder.

The people were aghast at the growing number of mice. "What are we to do?" they asked in terror. "They will eat up everything we have. And after we starve to death, they will eat our very flesh and bones."

R' Pinchas hushed them and motioned them to remove their hands from their ears. Then he said something strange, "Listen for a moment to the mice. Can you understand what they are saying?"

The people smiled. "Do we know mice-talk? How can you expect us to understand their silly squeaking?"

R' Pinchas soothed them. "Yes, but I do understand what they are trying to say. They are telling you that you did not take proper tithe, *maaser* from your produce. That is why they were sent to punish you by eating up your harvest in the field and in your barns."

The people hung their heads in shame. R' Pinchas was right. They had not taken off the proper tenth, the required *maaser*. They looked up at R' Pinchas, begging for help. "Please, accept our guarantee that in the future we will give *maaser*. Show us exactly how to do it, for we do not know all of the laws."

R' Pinchas taught them exactly how to set aside the *maaser* from their produce according to the *halachah*. And when they had done so, the mice miraculously disappeared. Every last one of them, never to return!

(According to Tractate *Yerushalmi Demai 1:3, Midrash Devarim Rabbah Parashah 3)*